W9-DFO-289

THE CHURCH
NOBODY KNOWS

THE CHURCH
NOBODY KNOWS

The Shaping of the
Future Church

by Michael Rogness

AUGSBURG PUBLISHING HOUSE
MINNEAPOLIS, MINNESOTA

THE CHURCH NOBODY KNOWS

Copyright © 1971 Augsburg Publishing House

All rights reserved. No part of this book may be used or reproduced in any manner whatsoever without written permission except in the case of brief quotations embodied in critical articles and reviews. For information address Augsburg Publishing House, 426 South Fifth Street, Minneapolis, Minnesota 55415.

Library of Congress Catalog Card No. 71-135230
International Standard Book No. O-8066-1112-X

Scripture quotations are from the Revised Standard Version of the Bible, copyright 1946 and 1952 by the Division of Christian Education of the National Council of Churches.

Manufactured in the United States of America

270.82
R63c

Contents

178892

Preface

The visionary title of this book refers to the church of the future, the church toward which the work of the "ecumenical movement" is pointed. Nobody knows today exactly what this church will look like. To avoid disillusioning the reader who is hoping for a prophet's blueprint of this future church, I must warn here that I have not ventured such a prediction.

Rather I am writing for the person who is asking, "With all these different churches, how will any kind of unity ever be possible?" The book is intended for everyone who is wondering what this ecumenical movement is all about and where it is headed. I have sketched some of the avenues in which we are moving toward wider unity. Perhaps a person reading between the lines can stretch his imagination and form his own vision of the church in A.D. 2000.

The ecumenical movement is slowly but surely filtering into the parishes of our churches after being largely confined to scholars, church leaders, and committees. And it is here among the people and congregations themselves that the real focus of our efforts toward Christian unity must finally be, despite the activity on administrative levels.

As a pastor I was privileged to participate with my

congregation in its first steps toward ecumenical dialog with other churches in our area. It was a small community, Howard Lake, Minnesota, where virtually everyone knew everyone else, but the walls of church division still stood high. Yet the people of our parish, and in the others as well, sensed that the movement toward ecumenism, cooperation, and unity is a providential sign of our times, and they were eager to build solid ties of brotherhood with their fellow Christians in other churches.

This book is dedicated therefore to the people I have served, as well as to those I am now serving at First Lutheran in Duluth, Minnesota, and to all others who look on the ecumenical movement with interest, some curiosity, and maybe a little anxiety. May it contribute to their understanding of what is surely the work of the Spirit drawing us closer to each other.

I am also grateful that I had the time and opportunity to write these pages as a staff member of the Institute for Ecumenical Research, an ecumenical study center established by the Lutheran World Federation in Strasbourg, France.

1.

The Changing Church

> ". . . on this rock I will build my church,
> and the powers of death shall not prevail
> against it" (Matthew 16:18).

Everybody from layman to bishop finds himself bewildered at the feverish discussion and activity going on within and between churches today. We live in a confusing age in which the clamor for change seems to be the slogan and constant turmoil the by-product. What is worse, there is always someone insisting on changing precisely those things you or I like just as they are!

This mood is not confined to the church. The whole world seems to be in restless turmoil. As often as not politics is conducted in an atmosphere of denunciation; the economists are always worried; we fear the moral standards of society are crumbling; youth has gotten out of hand; art, music, and literature have gone bizarre. Things are not "what they used to be in the good old days"!

Part of the reason for this is that the pace of life and of change has accelerated. With the placid pace of past centuries new developments took years, even decades and centuries to creep in upon the accustomed flow of daily life. Now everything changes so fast that our heads spin.

The fantastic burst of scientific development separates us from our children, who are growing up in a different world.

Split-second news of the whole world gives knowledge of customs, ideals, and convictions far different from our own. We cannot stay isolated from the "outside world" anymore.

Jet planes whoosh us across the world in a few hours. With expanding travel we have increased contact with "foreigners."

The widening gap between the rich and the poor within and between countries has produced explosive situations.

The underlying feeling of anxiety and nervousness in knowing that man can blot out millions by pushing buttons has affected the total population.

In the midst of this panorama of change, progress, anxiety, and opportunity, the church too is finding its way. Coinciding with the onrush of the modern world at the turn of this century was a resurging desire for Christian unity among Christian leaders and a feeling that the divisions and battles between various Christian churches were unchristian and discredited the church's work. What kind of Christian witness to brotherly love is it when Christians are constantly picking at each other? The Christian church awoke to find itself scoffed at by the cold eye of the outside world. Family fights are bad enough in the living room with the shades pulled, but now in the modern world when all the neighbors are peeking in, they are thoroughly shameful.

The modern world makes efforts toward unity an increasing necessity. Christians make up less than 30%

of the world population, a percentage steadily shrinking since the birth rate outstrips the "conversion rate." When you discover that you are part of a minority, your natural instinct is to pull together. It becomes obvious that our work in the world can be effective only if we are more united. In a sense, outside pressures are forcing us to do what the gospel has been urging for 2000 years.

But this new brotherhood is not just a defensive reaction of a minority group. This new situation has given us a fresh insight into our faith, that we are after all united in faith and through baptism to the triune God. Oliver Tomkins, Anglican bishop of Bristol, England, says that today "more and more Christians who live separated church lives are finding themselves compelled to admit that other Christians are indeed 'in Christ.'"[1] After concentrating on our differences for so many years, we now are rediscovering our common ground. In its *Decree on Ecumenism* the second Vatican Council takes note of the separations between churches and the "serious obstacles to full ecclesiastical communion" but affirms this bond of faith in Christ:

> Nevertheless all those justified by faith are incorporated into Christ through baptism. They therefore have a right to be honored by the title of Christian, and are properly regarded as brothers in the Lord . . .[2]

Ultimately the "ecumenical movement" is the desire to recapture the spirit of the New Testament church, which was one church despite its diverse elements. It is the yearning for the fulfillment of Christ's prayer in the Garden of Gethsemane:

> The glory which thou hast given me I have given to
> them, that they may be one even as we are one,
> I in them and thou in me, that they may become
> perfectly one . . . (John 17:22-23)

The movement was born with leaders of distant vision and vibrant hope, and now both their vision and their hope have borne fruit. On the international level we might date the beginning of the ecumenical movement with the World Missionary Conference at Edinburgh in 1910. The result of this gathering was the founding in 1921 of the International Missionary Council, which sponsored more conferences in Jerusalem, Madras, Whitby (Canada), and Willingen (Germany).

The impulses from Edinburgh produced two parallel movements. "Life and Work" was begun largely by the efforts of Archbishop Nathan Söderblom of Sweden and took as its motto, "Doctrine divides, service unites." It was launched in 1925 with a conference in Stockholm and continued with another conference twelve years later in Oxford. Yet those who were seeking unity through mission and through service realized that the divisive doctrinal issues could not be ignored, and "Faith and Order" began with a conference at Lausanne, Switzerland, in 1927. But it was soon apparent that the parallel roads to unity through mission, service, and doctrine could not run separately. The delegates of Faith and Order at Edinburgh in 1937 and those of Life and Work meeting simultaneously at Oxford agreed to merge their movements. This union was postponed by the war, but at Amsterdam in 1948 they formed the World Council of Churches, and at the historic WCC assembly in New Delhi in 1961 the trio became complete as the International Missionary Council merged with the WCC.

This sketch deals only with the ecumenism of international agencies, the tip of an immense iceberg. Today there are organizations, agencies, and committees of churches working together in every country of the world. Official conversations between church bodies are too numerous to mention, and unofficial meetings between teachers, pastors, and laymen of differing church traditions are countless. Universities and seminaries are setting up ecumenical lectures, courses, seminars, and professors' chairs to keep current.

The 1960s also marked the full participation of both the Orthodox and Roman Catholic churches in the ecumenical movement. The Orthodox became members of the World Council at the New Delhi assembly and have provided an energetic voice for their tradition. The second Vatican Council made it clear that Rome too was part of the ecumenical spirit, not only with the abundant hospitality lavished on non-Roman Catholic observers, but with its *Decree on Ecumenism* which recognized other churches as "churches" and opened new possibilities for dialog and cooperation with all Christendom.

We lack the space to chronicle the history of ecumenism, a story as fascinating as a novel. The interested reader can find these developments well described in many other books.[3] Rather we shall inquire about what is happening in all these meetings. What is an organization like the World Council doing? What happens at meetings of representatives between two churches? What are they aiming at? If differences between churches are disappearing, have we been wrong in our various faiths all these centuries? Where is it all heading, and will I like the result? In short, what is this "ecumenical movement"?

Two common misconceptions require attention. The first underestimates the ecumenical movement, the second misunderstands it. Both are common notions among church members.

The first idea is that the ecumenical movement aims to increase friendship and brotherhood between churches. But this is only the beginning, only a small part of what is involved. Yet what a necessary beginning! Any reader over 40 (in some places 25 or younger!) can remember the day when the Protestant minister and the Roman Catholic priest had nothing to do with each other. A story told by Cardinal Cushing of Boston reflects the wide-spread feeling of not so long ago. His predecessor once asked a priest in one of the diocese's most rundown, deprived parishes how things were going. "Badly, very badly, your eminence," was the answer, "but then, thank God, the Protestant churches are doing worse." [4] Even fellow Protestants kept their distance from one another. Such rancor has not totally disappeared, but it is happily now the exception, not the rule, and becoming increasingly rare.

In all but the most intransigent areas pastors and priests now consider themselves partners instead of combatants. This new friendliness is not just a polite courtesy, avoiding the thorny problems of religion. We are confident enough of our common Christian bond so that we can openly discuss even the most divisive issues. We are not playing a tense card game with our cards held tight against our chest, but we lay them flat out on the table in open and free conversation. The problems are still there, but the atmosphere is no longer hostile.

There is something marvelous in this! It is the difference between two new acquaintances who nervously guard every remark to keep the waters smooth and two old friends who no longer have to worry about offending one another. There are, of course, still those who are not receptive to this kind of openness, but the number is shrinking.

The same is happening among church members. Groups within congregations are taking steps to meet and work with groups of other congregations. Church leaders are not so worried about protecting their people from alluring new ideas, but see the value in broadening their views. "Living room dialogs" are becoming commonplace. A community is no longer automatically divided along church lines. Protestants are no longer unconsciously Republicans, and Roman Catholics can no longer be counted safe by the Democrats.

This new sense of friendship is both a product and a prerequisite of the ecumenical movement. After all, you can hardly discuss anything openly with somebody you think is "out to get you"! Dialog assumes trust in the integrity and good-will of the other partner. Such trust does not in itself reduce the differences between the churches, but it is the only basis on which we can understand one another.

But it would be quite incorrect to think of the ecumenical movement merely as a recovery of friendship between churches. Ecumenism has the more far-reaching goal of unity in one form or another. The bonds of trust and good-will are not the goal of ecumenism but rather its starting-point.

The other misleading idea of the ecumenical movement is that it is like horse-trading in which each side gives a little and takes a little, and then we come to agreement. If the Catholics are willing to give up the infallibility of the pope and let priests marry, for example, the Protestants will accept bishops and have their ministers say the Roman mass wearing full liturgical robes, and we shall all come about even. After all, if each side thinks it has been right all these years, will we not have to give up something to get together?

This attitude, whether conscious or unconscious, is the cause of much apprehension toward the ecumenical movement among our church people. They are quite naturally worried about what their leaders might "give up" and are anxious that some "ecumeniac" might be willing to surrender far too much for union. Bishop Tomkins describes this opposition to ecumenism:

> Basically the reason is fear. We are afraid that we shall compromise truth; afraid that we shall lose what is precious; afraid that we shall be expected to repudiate the grace of God in our past history; afraid that our distinctive witness will be smothered in an alien ethos; afraid that we shall have to accept ideas or institutions which our whole emotional (even more than mental) training has taught us to reject.[5]

It is not surprising that many people have this suspicion of ecumenical meetings. For example, we all know that the doctrine of the Lord's Supper has been an area of sharp, apparently irreconcilable contention between the Roman Catholics, Lutherans, and Reformed. Is it not certain to sound strange when scholars of these groups today say that the differences are no longer so overwhelming and were often caused by misunderstanding? If the differences are so small, how have they lasted so long? And if they are based on misunderstanding, why has somebody not cleared them up long ago? Or are these scholars so eager for unity that they are whitewashing very real differences?

These are good questions, and inevitable questions.

One main reason for this book is to answer such questions. This fear may not often be expressed, but it haunts the back corners in the minds of many who follow the ecumenical movement in their church papers. They are wondering whether in this world of swift changes forces are eroding away the foundations of their church and their faith. Their fear comes not from a lack of faith, but from the genuine concern of a strong faith.

The late Congregationalist ecumenical leader Douglas Horton reassured his readers:

> The first fact to remember is that in the whole vocabulary of ecumenism there are no such words as "surrender" or "compromise." . . . In the economy of ecumenizing there is no barter, no canceling of one belief or procedure held dear if the negotiator on the opposite side will cancel one of his. Those who hope that Rome may give up something she believes in, or that the Protestant world, independently or reciprocally, will give up some tenet or other, simply do not know what they are talking about.[6]

The ecumenical movement is not a watering down but an enrichment of our faith through deepening fellowship with our brothers.

What sort of unity does ecumenism seek? A huge united world church? Regional or national churches cooperating with one another? An acceptance of one another's churches as truly Christian? A mutual recognition of one another's sacraments and ministries? We do not know. The church of the future is described by the title of this book, "the church nobody knows," for only the Spirit knows where he is guiding his church.

Our task is to deal with the problems at hand right now, to attempt to clear up centuries of misunderstanding, to understand each other's convictions, and to try to realize what unity we have. An ecumenist is not one who pushes away all church barriers as unimportant; rather he is one who sees some problems as presently insurmountable, perhaps, but who is also compelled to see those of other churches as brothers in Christ.

The key word is love. We are drawn together in love to one another by him who first loved us. The love which compels us can be summarized by the overarching love for God, our Lord and Father. It is he who summons us on our quest for unity. The ecumenical movement is the response to this divine love. Being bound to him, we cannot be anything but dissatisfied and distressed that we are not bound more closely to one another. Abbé Paul Couturier of Lyon, France, the founder of the Week of Prayer for Christian Unity each January, said simply, "If we are to unite, we must love. . . ."

We speak of love for our brothers, and we must also include the love of truth. We bring into ecumenical meeting these two sides of love, and herein lies the poignancy of dialog. We long for unity, but in our loyalty to our own theological inheritance, traditions, and convictions we cannot be satisfied with easy answers which might mask unresolved problems. Those who accuse ecumenical churchmen of compromising the truth are ignorant of what is taking place.

In 1946 churchmen met in Geneva to resume the planning toward the World Council of Churches which had been interrupted by the war. Three preachers bore witness from the pulpit of the St. Pierre church to the deep fellowship they had experienced during the

ravages of the war years. Martin Niemöller recalled
that on the day he was taken off to prison by the
Nazis his aged father reassured him, "Be of good
cheer, my son. Remember that there will be Christians
praying for you from Greenland to the Pacific Islands,"
a thought that sustained Niemöller during those bleak
years. A Chinese Christian then told how he had been
imprisoned in Shanghai by the Japanese. He discovered by chance that the Japanese prison guard was also
Christian, and these two men knelt together in that
cell for prayer as their countries were shedding blood
against each other.

The third speaker was the courageous bishop of
Oslo, Eivind Berggrav, who was kept under house
arrest in the forest for his part in the resistance. He
told how the old man who brought him rations once
whispered when the guards were not looking, "My
old woman and I were listening to the BBC last night,
and we heard the Archbishop of Canterbury pray for
you by name." Berggrav concluded, "God has been
saying to us Christians in these war years, 'My Christians, you are one.'" Bishop Tomkins concludes these
episodes by adding, "In that spirit, the World Council
was born. It had to be!" [7]

Yes, ours is a world of change, and the church is in
the middle of it. Yet it is not a time for anxiety over
the change, but a time to rejoice in the opportunity
and summons to correct the mistakes of the past and
to renew the church for its work in the future. How
often we take a purely defensive stance, as if the
survival of the church depends on how much we
can cling to from the old days. Can we not face the
uncharted future with confidence in the promise of
the Lord of the church, who assured us that he will
hold his church fast, even against the powers of death?

Nobody has more cause to lose sleep over worry than the Roman Catholic pope, leader of the majority of the world's Christians. When Angelo Roncalli assumed these immense burdens as Pope John XXIII, he used to comfort himself at night with the thought,

"But who governs the Church? You or the Holy Spirit? Very well then, go to sleep, Angelo."[8]

2.

What's Going On?

. . . it is precisely while the community of peoples and nations was breaking asunder that the leaders of the Christian churches of the world have been drawing closer and closer together until they are today in fact more nearly united in understanding, in mutual trust, and even in organization for common action than ever before in Christian history.[*]

— Henry P. Van Dusen

Thus far the 20th century has seen the nations of the world repeatedly torn apart in bloody conflict. Yet at the same time the Christian church has discovered a fellowship among its many members which is steadily growing. Several factors draw us together as we study, discuss, and work with each other.

For centuries Roman Catholics have regarded Protestants as heretics and schismatics, and Protestants have in turn looked on the Roman church as a corruption of biblical faith. But now that we have become accustomed to rub shoulders with one another, we realize that what we have in common is far more extensive than the disagreements separating us. After all, just in saying the Apostles' Creed together, Christians from all churches share the basic essentials of Christianity. Let us not inflate the remaining differences out of proportion! One expression of this change in climate came from Pope John XXIII:

> What unites us is far more important than what separates us in this cause which is so noble and so useful, namely to reestablish the bonds of concord in the unity of the one pure faith.

Our differences have not vanished into thin air, but now we at least come together as brothers in Christ rather than opponents.

We must note immediately the very crucial fact that *Christians from many churches are now studying the Bible together.* Prof. K. E. Skydsgaard, Danish Lutheran observer at the Vatican Council, points out how significant it is that Roman Catholics and Protestant scholars "go about their task of reading the Bible without their confessional spectacles and without constantly squinting at their doctrinal prejudices." [10]

Today more and more Christians are reading the Bible as the source of church life and renewal rather than as an arsenal of ammunition against other churches. All reputable biblical scholars today read the studies of men from other churches. Earlier a bitterly contested battleground, Bible study has now become a resource for unity. Dr. W. A. Visser 't Hooft, the Dutch ecumenical leader, told the World Council of Churches Central Committee in 1966 that "the secret force driving us together has been the biblical *kerygma* [Gospel message] which we have again heard in a new way on both sides." A young Swedish professor recently deplored that cooperation among dogmatic theologians is still an "underdeveloped territory" compared to the work of biblical scholars.

A side effect of this new situation is that the attitude of "according-to-the-Bible-I'm-right-and-you're wrong" does not convince very many people. Such sweeping self-confidence which paints the picture only in black and white is not realistic. It is hardly reasonable to insist that I am absolutely "right" and others of equal or more intelligence, learning, devotion, and faith are "wrong." The sight of many churches, wherein every group claims exclusive possession of the truth, strikes any sensible observer as ridiculous.

Does it logically follow then, that if nobody is absolutely right, then we are all wrong? If nobody is right, is there no truth? Must assurance be replaced by doubt and confusion? No, this is not the case. Rather, we are realizing that "truth" is something more than a series of propositions we defend. We are realizing that truth cannot be neatly packaged and bound into textbooks, though textbooks are indispensable. And this realization gives us an expanded and fresh perspective on the Bible itself.

Now we read the Scriptures in a different light. We are more aware that an author was writing for a particular situation, or to a particular group of people. His comments were shaped by those circumstances, and we must be careful that we are not applying his words to a totally different situation. For instance, Paul writes to the Galatians that "a man is not justified by works of the law but through faith in Jesus Christ." James, on the other hand, writes that "a man is justified by works and not by faith alone." For centuries these verses have been used as clubs by Protestants and Catholics against each other. But are they really so contradictory? Paul asserts the primacy of faith against those who insist on the Jewish law for Christians, whereas James confronts the perennial problem of an inactive, lazy faith with the admonition that faith must be a living thing. A theologian who stretches these verses into two different doctrines of justification is hardly taking note of the situation in which each author writes. Time and time again it has become clear that we have used passages against other churches by taking them out of their context.

We have learned to acknowledge that most of what we teach and do ("theology" and "practice") in the church is determined from the history or tradition of our denominations. Indeed, even the most basic elements of the Christian church were decided long after the Bible had been finished. The office of the ministry is an example. During the first decades after Jesus' resurrection, when the disciples were still living and writing the New Testament, only rudimentary beginnings were made toward church organization. And they were aimed at meeting the needs at hand rather than conforming to any predetermined structure. The Bible does not and can not dictate answers to all problems of church organization, because some of these situations had not yet arisen in biblical times.

Another instance is the practice of baptism. In the New Testament we read only of adult and "household" baptisms (Acts 16:15, 1 Cor. 1:16) never of infant baptisms. Yet infants were presumably baptized as part of the household, and we know that in the decades following the completion of the New Testament books infants born into Christian homes were baptized.

Almost all the topics of ecumenical discussion fall into this category: the Bible gives us general guidelines, but doctrine and practice were developed more exactly through the years. Worship services, church structure, the relation of church and state — all of these and more evolved in the history of the church. Inevitably they developed differently from one place to another, until finally they became sources of dispute and division.

Therefore we probe the historical development of our dogmas and doctrines. How and why did they assume the shape they did? What circumstances of history played a role in determining them? How did it happen that the church expressed its convictions about Christ in the particular words of the Nicene Creed? Why did it happen that the Roman church officially fixed the number of sacraments at the traditional seven in 1547 after the reformers had reduced the number to two, when the word "sacrament" is not in the Bible anyway?

Though a doctrine might not be fully expressed in the Bible, did it develop in harmony with the spirit or concern of the Bible, or does it grow so far removed from the Scriptures that it violates the spirit of the Bible? A Baptist poses this question to those who hold a complex doctrine of infant baptism, a Protestant to a Roman Catholic concerning his loyalty to the pope, a Roman Catholic to a Congregationalist for his rejection of bishops, or a Pentecostal to other churches for skipping lightly over the work of the Holy Spirit, and so on. In short, is our way of thinking and doing consistent with the biblical intent, or have we strayed? An Anglican professor at Oxford expresses this principle in writing about the liturgy:

> What are the reasons for wanting change in the liturgy? The first comes from the New Testament. In important respects our Holy Communion service is poles apart from the New Testament teaching. The New Testament men did and taught one thing and we do and teach another. It is true, but no comfort to point out, that other liturgies are not better. We must try to mend our own. So I set out

to discover what a New Testament liturgy might
look like and to bring our service into line with
the teaching of the Bible.[11]

In reading 1 Corinthians 11, for example, you will
immediately see what Mr. Kilpatrick means, that the
Lord's Supper celebration in the early church was
vastly different from that of any church today.

We ask: Are the differences between us enough to
justify our separations? The Christian faith is profoundly personal, and there will always be personal
differences. But at what point do I say, "I find that
your ideas are so diverse from mine that I cannot be in
the same church with you"? Or when can I say, "If
those are the only differences between us, there is no
reason for our churches to be separated"? Must a
Lutheran say to a Presbyterian, "Yes, we both believe
in Christ's real presence in the Lord's Supper, but you
explain it differently, so I refuse to go to your Communion service, and you please stay away from mine"?

There were certainly many differences in the early
church, and yet that church was one and united. The
worship life of the various churches developed rather
independently of one another. To use another example again, though Paul and James may not have been
flatly contradictory, neither were their respective theological views identical. In terms of structure, less than
a century after Pentecost, Bishop Ignatius of Antioch
was insisting on a bishop with full authority, while at
the same time other churches were more democratic.
But with all this variety there was no talk of these
parties splitting off and starting new churches.

To press the point further, at what point do I no
longer say, "This is a different opinion from mine, but
still Christian," but rather, "This is not Christian; it is

heresy, and I want nothing to do with you!"? Where do we draw the line between another Christian opinion and an evil, unchristian heresy? This might sound like a very academic question, but it is crucial for us all. Many people are convinced that their opinion is so right and others so wrong that dialog has no value whatsoever.

Last comes a factor which is rapidly becoming the most important of them all. There are many questions we ask together, which are entirely apart from our confessional differences. All of us — Catholic, Protestants, Orthodox, Anglican, or Pentecostal — are asking how the church can best serve in our technological, secular society. How does the Christian church bring meaning to a worker on an automated mass assembly line? What is the Christian ethic in the business world? In the slum areas of our urban centers? These are new problems, so our approach to them is not burdened by past controversies.

In fact, an increasing number of younger churchmen openly admit that they are not much interested in tedious ecumenical dialog over traditional problems of the past when the needs of today's society present such an immense challenge to the church. "Let the dead bury their own dead," they say of the old controversies and carry out their work virtually ignoring the divisions which separate them from others.

Now when churchmen look at the issues in view of all these factors, what is likely to happen? How can consensus be found after a series of discussions on problems which have divided us for centuries?

As I have said, for most church members this question is a real puzzler. Roman Catholics worry that their scholars are selling out to the Protestants, and Protestants are left with the alternatives that either the Reformers were wrong or today's ecumenical leaders are willing to water down Reformation truths in favor of a patch-up unity job. How is it, then, that these problems are "solved"?

Theological divisions are in fact confronted and resolved, or "solved" in several ways. We have already seen how joint Bible study throws controversial issues into new perspectives. The following pages will explain some of the ways by which ecumenical dialog clears up misunderstandings and disagreements.

By meeting in an atmosphere of trust after centuries of mistrust, we often discover that our understanding of others is no more than a twisted caricature. Long years of sour feelings have caused us to see only the worst in other churches. The end result was some flagrantly ridiculous ideas. A Catholic friend, for example, was astounded to learn that Protestants had sacraments! On the other hand, Protestants had so inflated their notions of Roman Catholic priestly and papal power that thousands were worried that American policy would be dictated from Rome following the inauguration of John F. Kennedy.

Some of our false ideas are deeply rooted. At one Roman Catholic-Protestant consultation the participants devised a scheme to insure that each side would clearly understand the other. After a lecture one member of the other tradition summarized what had just been said. One would think it would be simple enough to repeat and condense what was said with practically no chance of misleading interpretation. Yet the lecturers found that they were continually "correcting" their interpreters.

The late Jesuit ecumenical pioneer, Gustave Weigel, once wrote,

> It would be silly to ask non-Catholics to share the Catholic church's view of herself, but it would be disastrous if they were not to know it. If we are to speak to each other, we should know how each partner of the conversation appears to himself.[12]

With centuries of cultivated misunderstanding behind us, the first thing we must do is to listen, listen carefully and exactly. In ecumenical dialog the little proverb carries much truth: "I never learned anything with my mouth open"!

Merely clarifying definitions of the same word can open new avenues of agreement. Frequently scholars of one tradition use a word quite differently from others. One of the most familiar and frequently used phrases heard in ecumenical discussion is the comment, "Well if that's what you mean, then . . ."

A classic example is the word "substance," which was the focal point of great battles in the Reformation between German Lutherans and Swiss Reformed. The question was: is Christ *substantially* present in the Lord's Supper? The Lutherans understood "substance" to mean that which makes something what it is, as "the substance of an argument." So of course the substance of Christ is present in the Supper, otherwise he would not be there at all. The Swiss thought of substance in more concrete terms: the "substance" of a table is wood. Since Christ does not come back down from heaven as the same man of flesh and blood he once was each time the Supper is celebrated, one cannot say he is "substantially" present in the Eucharist.

Upon hearing this denial, the Lutherans accused the Swiss of denying the very presence of Christ itself. The Swiss on the other hand charged the Lutherans with some kind of superstitious cannibalism as bad as anything taught by the medieval Roman church. How tragic for the course of the Reformation that both sides did not pause back at the beginning and get straight what they meant by the word "substance"!

But we trip over words just as often today. How many churches have been wracked with controversy over the question of "biblical inspiration," or "biblical inerrancy"! But have the combatants ever sat down and first examined their definitions of "inspiration" before unleashing their artillery? Some hesitate to use the term "verbal inspiration" for fear that it will be understood as an impersonal stenographic, dictating process, quite apart from the faith of the apostles and the church. The other side rises up to defend the term, because for them it expressed the affirmation that the biblical books are indeed witnesses of faith guided by the Spirit of God. This affirmation might be held by both sides, but they have got themselves stuck in a muddle of words.

Naturally this does not mean that all disputes disappear when definitions are clarified. There were real differences between the Lutherans and the Swiss, and there are many variations in the understanding of "biblical inerrancy." But not until one understands exactly what the other means will the genuine disagreements be apparent. And it is more than likely that once the definitions are cleared up, the remaining contrasts will show up in a new light and likely be far less formidable than previously thought.

Sometimes we discover that another church is saying the same thing as we, only saying it in a different way. A church in a certain area, in a certain period of history, and confronting certain problems will naturally end up expressing itself differently from a church in other circumstances. The same truth of the gospel might be couched in a variety of expressions.

We know that "truth" and "theology" are not the same things. Truth is eternal and unchanging, but ways of explaining the truth arise from the needs and situations of the church. Jesus Christ is indeed "the same yesterday and today and for ever" (Heb. 13:8), but we have to proclaim his work through the ever-changing medium of human language. Therefore two churches might talk about a thing in sharply divergent fashions, while seeking to express the same conviction.

Let us look again at the doctrine of the Lord's Supper — and I must admit to using the Eucharist as a frequent example, since it has been the focus of such bitter battles. Protestants have traditionally plunged into heated combat at the mere mention of the Roman Catholic teaching of "transubstantiation," the doctrine that the "substance" of bread and wine is changed to Christ's body and blood, even though the "accidents" (externals of taste, smell, feel, appearance, etc.) remain the same. The Roman Catholic church formulated the doctrine when the intellectual atmosphere was Aristotelian and such concepts were commonly understood. But in subsequent centuries Protestants, who no longer thought as Aristotelians, saw the doctrine as some kind of farfetched unbiblical rationalization.

Now thanks to this ecumenical age Roman Catholic scholars have taken pains to explain to both Roman Catholics and Protestants the *intent* of this doctrine, namely that God really *does* something and that Christ really *is* present in the Lord's Supper. Furthermore, this intent is precisely the intent which most Protestants affirm.

When a joint committee of American Lutherans and

Roman Catholics met in 1966-1967, the Lutheran conclusion was the following:

> It becomes clear to them [Lutherans] that the
> dogmas of transubstantiation intends to affirm the
> fact of Christ's presence and of the change which
> takes place . . . when the dogma is understood in
> this way, Lutherans find that they also must ac-
> knowledge that it is a legitimate way of attempting
> to express the mystery. . . .

The Lutherans also added that they still felt this way
of thinking "is misleading and therefore prefer to
avoid the term." [13]

Naturally not all problems are automatically eliminated simply by understanding another person's intent
behind his language, just as it would be far too simple
and premature to say that Lutherans and Roman
Catholics have reached agreement on the Eucharist.
But we do discover how often we are trying to say
the same thing, but have become used to different
ways of saying it. The value of ecumenical dialog is
that we often get so used to our way of thinking that
we need another person to tell us that our accustomed
thought forms are not understood so well today. A
Roman Catholic can evaluate a Protestant idea as an
outsider, and vice versa, providing a rewarding source
of insight. Every church must constantly examine its
theology — how much more profitable to do it together!

*Ecumenical dialog only rarely deals with absolute
yes-no, either-or alternatives; more frequently each
side enriches the other.* As I mentioned before, each
tradition has developed its own perspectives. Since
these grew out of particular historical circumstances
for the church's need at the time, it is unavoidable
that in every tradition some viewpoints are stressed

at the expense of others. It would be quite presumptuous for a theologian to claim, "My tradition and my doctrine comprehend in perfect balance all aspects of the Christian faith."

In dialog we "pool our resources," so to speak. We learn from others; we see things in our faith which we had not appreciated or emphasized before. We share those particular teachings we hold dear in our own traditions. At the same time we discover where we may have overemphasized and underemphasized parts of the Christian faith.

Pick any ecumenical topic almost at random and this is the case. For example, the question of infant or adult baptism is about as clear-cut an "either-or" topic as there is in ecumenical discussion. You believe infants either should or should not be baptized. Yet even here each side can learn from the other, even though nobody knows what, if any, agreement on the matter will be reached in the future. The churches holding the traditional position of infant baptism have too often made baptism a formal, automatic ritual. They learn from those of Baptist conviction the necessity of faith within baptism, so that they stress more strongly the importance of the parents and godparents in bringing up the child in the faith into which he is baptized. The Baptists, on the other hand, believe in baptism only for those actually old enough to believe for themselves. But they take note from other traditions of the need to guard against the thought of faith and baptism as an accomplishment of man and to affirm continually that it is God who works faith and baptizes. Thus in the discussion of these presently unresolvable views each side does learn from the other.

This cross-fertilization is nowhere more obvious than observing the imposing presence of the Orthodox churches in the World Council of Churches. Protestants and Roman Catholics have been reheating their yesterday's polemics for over four hundred years. How refreshing it has been to hear an Orthodox theologian enter the discussion by saying, "Instead of both of you looking at it always that way, why not approach the question from this angle. . . ." Such experiences are enlightening for all sides.

One of the areas in which ecumenical dialog has been slow in coming is the meeting between the older churches and the "Pentecostal" churches. The Pentecostals have scorned other churches as spiritually dead and have themselves been looked upon as narrow and emotional anti-intellectuals. Ecumenical leaders have prayed and waited for the time when this large family of various churches would join the ecumenical stream, and now the barriers of mistrust show signs of cracking. It is certain that the Pentecostals have much to give to the other established groups, and that they can profit from wider contact.

Almost all of us have had the experience of worshipping in another church and thinking, "I like the way they do that." The ecumenical movement has opened our eyes to various forms and ways of worship other than our own. Those who come from churches with a rather formal liturgy have learned to appreciate the informality of other traditions. Those accustomed to freer worship services are impressed with the sense of reverence toward God's majesty in a highly liturgical service. As a result of these broadened horizons, all churches are constantly asking how their liturgical forms of worship might be improved. No one expects or hopes that all this will lead to one melted-down style of worship. But what will happen is that the worship life of each church can become richer by learning from others.

These are some of the ways the sharp edges of our theological and churchly differences are removed. Now that the reader has a glimpse into "what's going on" in ecumenical dialog, the next step is to examine the barriers that stand before us on the way to unity.

3.

What Unites? What Divides?

> My father is a member of the Holiness church,
> my mother is a Methodist, my brother is an
> Episcopalian, my wife is a Baptist, and I am a
> Congregationalist. Why are there such divisions
> in the family of God?
>
> —a plea from a young Japanese Christian

Christians have begun to grasp the pathos and the
urgent challenge embodied in this question from a
son of Christian missions in Japan. His is indeed the
central question of ecumenism.

Let us ask ourselves the deceptively simple question,
"What is it that unites us — and divides us?" The reader will reply immediately, "We are in the same church
because we are Lutheran. My neighbor is a Baptist,
so he belongs to a different church, and the same with
the Roman Catholic across the street and the Methodist I work with." That would be the logical answer,
one which we all take for granted.

But the problem becomes a bit more complex when
we start looking in back of the question. Why can
the church bodies of these neighbors not get together?
What prevents the Presbyterians and Methodists from
uniting, even though they disagree on some items?
There are disputes within every church which do not

necessarily cause it to split apart. Why is it not possible for the Roman Catholic and the Orthodox churches to merge, since they share such common bonds as apostolic succession and the same seven sacraments? What is holding back various church merger talks throughout the world? For that matter, why are churches of the same denomination often divided — in the United States, for example, the Lutherans, or Presbyterians, or Baptists?

What keeps us united? What forces divisions? Many complex factors are involved, but I shall break them down into three categories. Churches are united and have been divided:

   (a) by doctrine
   (b) by ministry and structure
   (c) by worship and piety

In the next three chapters we shall take a closer look at each of these, but first let us see exactly what they mean.

(a) Doctrine

This is the category which says, "I am united with the members of my church by the common doctrine we accept, and we are divided from other churches because they have different doctrine." We speak of "Roman Catholic doctrine," or "Lutheran doctrine," or "Calvinist doctrine" because traditions have handed down distinctive doctrinal positions.

The spark that ignited the Reformation was Martin Luther's conviction that the New Testament gospel of God's grace had been obscured. The Roman Catholic church of the Middle Ages, he insisted, had cluttered the clear gospel voice with all sorts of obstacles to a man's saving faith in God — indulgences, clergy, and papal dominance, superstitious practices, and church corruption. Luther's lifework, as he saw it, was to proclaim anew the biblical message that we are saved exclusively by the grace of God in Jesus Christ, given us through faith.

His co-workers and followers devoted themselves to preserving and explaining this "pure doctrine." The reformers (they were not called "Lutherans" then, and Luther would not like it now either) formulated their doctrinal convictions in the *Augsburg Confession* of 1530, Philip Melanchthon's *Apology* to the *Augsburg Confession* and finally in the *Formula of Concord.* These documents, plus Luther's catechisms, the ancient creeds and other statements comprise the *Book of Concord.* This volume defined the Lutheran doctrinal position against Rome, the Calvinists, and the smaller sectarian groups of the time (mainly Baptist). Their concern for uniform and pure doctrine has given the Lutherans at best a firm theological tradition, yet often at worst a relentless self-confidence in being right where others are wrong. As a result, Lutherans have developed a tendency to splinter themselves apart over doctrinal quarrels of all sorts.

So it is that Lutherans have always considered themselves a "doctrinal" or "confessional" church and have taken their theological position seriously. Such serious doctrinal interest has also produced within Lutheranism an uneasiness to become too involved ecumenically with churches of other doctrinal traditions. This characteristic dates back to the 1529 meeting between Luther and Zwingli at the Marburg castle. Because Zwingli did not accept Luther's formulation on the Lord's Supper, Luther refused to reach the hand of church fellowship to the Swiss reformer.

Actually the "official" Lutheran position is not narrow and was intended to be genuinely ecumenical. The *Augsburg Confession* explicitly rejects a total doctrinal uniformity as basis for church union:

> For the true unity of the church it is enough to agree concerning the teaching of the gospel and the administration of the sacraments.[14]

It would appear that Lutherans insist only on agreement in essential matters, as seems to be the intent of this statement. But the problem is that this sentence has proved wide open to drastically varying interpretations. For some the word "gospel" means the central message of forgiveness and reconciliation in Christ. Others stretch the word like an umbrella to cover every doctrinal implication, reasoning that all doctrinal matters are ultimately related to the gospel. This conservative position then takes the position that unless two church groups can agree on *all* points of doctrine they ought not to enter into union or even fellowship (receive each other's sacraments and listen to each other's sermons) with one another. The ultra-rigid attitude is slowly giving way to the realization that neither the biblical nor the Reformation church intended such sweeping uniformity, but it still plagues efforts of Lutheran ecumenism.

Lutherans have taken doctrinal strictness quite for granted. All merger negotiations involving Lutherans are preceded by exhaustive discussions to determine whether adequate doctrinal consensus exists. If it does, the major roadblock to unity or fellowship is removed. But if such negotiations uncover doctrinal disagreement — and sometimes relatively peripheral issues are magnified into essential doctrine — the Lutherans bow out of such negotiations. This means that Lutherans have never taken part in non-Lutheran Protestant mergers. When the Church of South India was formed in 1947 between Presbyterian, Methodist, Congregationalist, and Anglican churches, the Lutherans stayed away because the union was not on the basis of the Lutheran confessions. The largest Protestant union in history is now underway in the United States between Episcopalians, Methodists, Presbyterians, United Church of Christ, and others (Consultation on Church Union — COCU), but the Lutherans remain on the sidelines as spectators because the doctrine of the proposed church will not be expressly Lutheran. In short, Lutherans will discuss doctrine with anybody, but they have shown only minimal interest in merger or closer fellowship with non-Lutheran churches. Two exceptions are the Lutheran Church of Sweden which has fellowship with the Anglican Church of England, and a number of European Lutheran churches who have fellowship with Reformed-Presbyterian churches.

Lutherans provide the best example of unity and division because of doctrine. They have never been greatly concerned about the other two factors in ecumenical relations — ministry and structure, or worship and piety. In these latter two areas Lutherans display a surprising flexibility. They do not have a fixed position on ministry and structure — perhaps we should say more accurately that they have several positions. American Lutherans are congregational with church presidents, many European Lutherans are hierarchical with bishops, and some even have archbishops (Swedes, Finns, Estonians, Latvians). Swedish Lutheran pastors are ordained in the continuity of apostolic-episcopal succession, but other Lutherans consider apostolic succession unnecessary to the ministry of the church.

Nor is there any "Lutheran" church structure. Among Lutheran churches throughout the world one can find examples of almost every structure possible.

Neither do Lutherans insist on any single type of worship or piety. There is no such thing as an exclusively "Lutheran" liturgy. In most countries, Lutheran liturgy is simply a condensation of the traditional Roman mass, with all sorts of variations. Such things as vestments are also varied. Some Lutheran pastors put on several layers of robes for worship, while a few content themselves with a business suit. Americans usually wear a surplice with a colorful stole, while most European Lutherans wear somber black. Indeed, the *Augsburg Confession* expressly states that:

> it is not necessary that human traditions or rites and ceremonies, instituted by men, should be alike everywhere. (Article 7)

For Lutherans, therefore, ministry and structure or worship and piety are not the issues over which the church is united or divided. Divisions are based on doctrine and can be overcome only by doctrinal agreement.

But of course Lutherans are not the only ones for whom unity and separations are measured by doctrine. To become a Roman Catholic means to accept a number of officially stated dogmas and doctrinal traditions. Between Roman Catholics and Protestants stand an imposing lineup of doctrinal obstacles to unity. Strict Calvinists and Presbyterian Reformed groups also take their doctrine seriously and will not unite with others when doctrinal differences persist.

Ultimately every church has some kind of doctrinal position. Baptists are fond of claiming adherence to no dogmas, just the "Bible alone," but their rejection of infant baptism is for all practical purposes a doctrine that keeps them separated from those who do baptize infants. Even groups that disclaim all dogma, such as Congregationalists or Quakers, hold certain convictions that correspond to doctrinal positions. We shall take a closer look at this area of doctrine in the next chapter.

(b) Ministry and Structure

The Christian church has a plethora of offices: pastors, priests, bishops, elders, councilmen, deacons, trustees, presidents, chairmen, clerks, cardinals, etc., and once even three popes at the same time! It operates with an infinite number of organizational forms. The problems of ministry (office, function, authority of pastors, priests, and bishops) and structure (organization of the church) are almost too vast and complex to be pressed together into one section, but they are also too intertwined to be separated. Any discussion concerning the unity and divisions of the church soon finds itself deeply entangled in these matters.

Anybody speaking with an Anglican (Episcopalian) finds himself skipping rather quickly over questions of doctrine and landing on such topics as ministry, bishops, and apostolic succession. An Anglican would not likely split a church on doctrinal issues. A look at the vast span in doctrine and practice between the "high church" Anglicans, who are almost indistinguishable from Roman Catholics (hence their name "Anglo-Catholics"), all the way to the "low church" groups, often indistinguishable from the free churches, boggles the orderly mind of a Lutheran who thinks of a church as one with a consistent doctrinal outlook. It also baffles anybody who considers church unity in terms of a common way of worship.

The Anglicans of the world are united around their ministry. The "Anglican Communion" is the worldwide fellowship of Anglicans who are bound together by one single thread: Anglican bishops in all countries and continents recognize the Archbishop of Canterbury as their symbol of unity. He has little actual authority over the other bishops, but since he has historically been the "senior bishop" among Anglicans, he retains an enormous prestige as Anglican leader. There is no world-wide Anglican church organization. Every ten years or so Anglican bishops the world over journey to the Archbishop of Canterbury's residence at the Lambeth palace in London for a "Lambeth Conference," where the affairs of the Anglican Communion are discussed. This unity around the bishops and the Archbishop of Canterbury is the bond which holds Anglican-Episcopalians together.

The Anglican church was not formed from doctrinal convictions, as was the Lutheran church. It began soon after the German Reformation when Henry VIII decided that the church in England would no longer give allegiance to the pope in Rome. The king of England became the nominal head of the Church of England, and the Archbishop of Canterbury was recognized as ecclesiastical head. The whole English Church (with some notable exceptions like Sir Thomas More) was converted by decree, so to speak, to Anglicanism. As the years went by Reformation ideas from Wittenberg and Geneva took root, so that the brief creedal statement of the "39 Articles" is more Protestant than Roman. But a wide spectrum of doctrinal outlook has always prevailed among Anglicans.

When an Anglican talks with a Lutheran, he will not be overly interested in the contents of the *Book of Concord*. He will more likely want to know if the

Lutheran ministry is "valid." The Lutherans ordain men who are trained in theology and Lutheran doctrine without paying much attention to whether he is ordained by a bishop who stands in the line of apostolic succession. But such things are important to an Anglican, because he values the unbroken continuity with the bishopric office from the ancient church and believes that Lutherans have broken this line. It is for this reason that the Anglican Church of England recognizes fellowship with the Lutheran church in Sweden, because the Swedish Lutheran bishops have retained this continuous line.

After years of patient work toward a reunion between the Anglican and Methodist churches in England, the Anglicans failed in 1969 to give a large enough majority vote to go ahead. Why? Mainly because the high-church party was not satisfied with the plan for reconciling the ministries of the two churches. The Anglican-United Church of Canada union talks balanced delicately on questions of ministry, a main problem being the Anglican unwillingness to accept the ordained women pastors in the United Church.

This question of ministry and authority is also the major problem between the Roman Catholics and Orthodox. From a purely doctrinal point of view Rome is much closer to the Orthodox than to Protestants. The stumbling block is the claim of the Roman pope to be the supreme authority over all the other bishops, a claim the Orthodox will not accept.

Another, perhaps the best, example of division caused by ministry and authority is between the Roman Catholics and the "Old Catholic churches," who consider themselves fully Catholic but not Roman, since they too reject the supremacy and infallibility of the Roman pope. In (a) doctrine and (c) worship and piety they appear practically identical with Roman Catholicism. But it is this second level of ministry and structure which divides them. Contrast these groups with the "Uniate" churches. These are distinct from Roman Catholicism with Greek as their theological language and with their own liturgical traditions, but they are counted in the Roman Catholic fold because they do accept the bishop of Rome as pope (although they zealously guard their own ecclesiastical rights).

On the whole I would consider the Roman Catholic church primarily in this (b) category, which is to say that the predominant mark of unity in the Roman Catholic church today is loyalty to the hierarchical ministry, the structure of bishops with the pope at the head. It was formerly true that a uniform doctrinal point of view was the mark of Roman Catholic cohesion, but that is no longer as true today, although Roman Catholicism does have continual and consistent doctrinal viewpoints. In theory the Roman Catholics speak of accepting the whole body of traditional dogma handed down through the history of their church, and we Protestants have pictured Roman Catholic believers and theologians as burdened with a smothering weight of "official" dogma which they are obligated to accept. But such a picture is simply not realistic today. Perhaps it was once, when many theologians repeated the tried and true formulas of days past. But that day is no more. A Roman Catholic scholar will accept his church's teaching of seven sacraments, for instance, but within that framework today's scholars have found an enormous amount of elbow room for fresh interpretation. Roman Catholic theologians are as free and adventuresome today as

any and are generally counted as loyal Roman Catholics, as long as they — and this is the crucial part —
consider themselves loyal to their bishop and to the
pope. Many Roman Catholics disagree with the pope
on the matter of birth control, for example, but are still
loyal to him as the chief shepherd of the church and
are therefore considered true members of the Roman
church.

The same is true of worship and piety. Roman Catholics used to be a uniform group, with the Latin mass
reigning all over the world. Though the mass still binds
Roman Catholic worshippers with one another, now
it is celebrated with much variety across the world,
and this variety is sure to increase in years to come.
I once preached regularly in a small army chapel. Our
Protestant service with its traditional hymns played in
traditional style on an organ was followed by a Roman
Catholic mass in which a New York nun played contemporary music with guitar accompaniment. It is
clear that different forms of piety and worship will be
developing in Roman Catholicism, so that any one
way of worship or piety will not be the main unifying
mark within the church of Rome.

Yet in spite of the growing theological diversity and
the renewal in worship forms the Roman Catholic
church is one church. Why? Because all its elements
retain their loyalty to the ministry and structure of the
church. Those priests, theologians, and others who
leave the Roman church do so principally because
they can no longer live within the structure, authority,
and regulations of the Roman Catholic church. This is
the critical issue within Roman Catholicism today.
But ultimately these are key problems for all churches,
and we shall look at them more closely in a following
chapter.

(c) Worship and Piety

I have used these vague terms "worship and piety" as a catch-all phrase to describe the general "feel" of a church's spiritual life. Every church has a distinctive personality or "style of life" apart from its doctrinal statements or ministerial organization. A Protestant attending a Russian Orthodox mass finds himself in a completely foreign, almost exotic, atmosphere, and a Roman Catholic feels utterly strange in a Baptist revival meeting.

This dimension is very important in ecumenical relationships. It may prove the most difficult barrier of all to overcome. A Presbyterian might feel somewhat at home in a Lutheran or Methodist church, but in a Greek mass he would likely feel quite ill at ease or lost. If church leaders were to announce a church union between Roman Catholics and Southern Baptists — hardly an imminent possibility! — such a union would amount to no more than a piece of paper, because the two churches are so enormously different in their ways of life and worship. How can we speak of fellowship and union between churches whose piety, way of worship, or "feel" is so incompatible?

These differences in practice and piety have many sources. Theology plays an important role in forming the life of a church. The theology of the Roman Catholic church has, for instance, laid heavy emphasis on the sacraments, so it is natural that the Roman worship and church life should focus strongly on the sacraments. The Reformation, on the other hand, stressed the importance of gospel proclamation and congregational participation, so Protestant worship has come to emphasize Scripture reading, preaching and hymn singing.

Theology does play a role, but not the predominant

role in shaping a church's way of worship. The church's cultural heritage makes a decisive contribution to this development. Latin became the language of the Roman Catholic church because it was the universal language of the Roman empire. The Orthodox tradition is more Greek because eastern Mediterranean intellectual life centered around the Greek language. In church music we think of Roman Catholicism in terms of Gregorian chants (though less so today) and the Protestants with their chorales. These reflect the historical settings of these traditions, though now we sing each other's songs. Liturgies in general are mixed products of theology and culture.

A church's national background is an important factor in its piety and life, especially in the United States, where so many of our churches were started by newly arrived immigrants. Sometimes the church represented an extension of the old country, and the new Americans tried to preserve their folk customs in their parishes. The worship scene in midwestern America in the late 1800s was a veritable land of Babel, where prayers might be uttered in several European languages within a single county. With the maturing of the post-war generation, the process of "Americanization" is virtually complete, but the various churches still retain many worship characteristics of their forefathers.

For whatever the reason, the fact remains that there is a boundless variety of "worship and piety" in the Christian church. It reflects the richness of the church, but it also represents a real challenge to the ecumenical movement. How can we prevent this variety from splitting and estranging us even further? How can we feel Christian fellowship with those whose worship style is totally alien to us? When the differences are so vast, should we not just "live and let live" apart from each other, since we probably shall not understand strange churches anyway?

(d) Social Factors

These first three areas by which churches are united and divided are all genuinely religious in nature. But we must face the fact that non-religious social factors have played a discouragingly large part in the church and its unity.

The apostle Paul set before the young Christian church a splendid vision of a unity in Christ that would cut through and shatter all the earthly fences that keep us from one another:

> There is neither Jew nor Greek, there is neither slave nor free, there is neither male nor female; for you are all one in Christ Jesus. (Gal. 3:28)

But the church has proved all too human after all, and this vision has been repeatedly violated by church groups which turn out to embrace a certain class, race, economic group, or type of people. Middle class people generally belong to middle class churches, where neither the very poor nor even the very rich feel warmly received. Whites worship almost exclusively with whites, blacks with blacks, and an Indian or Chinese would probably feel unwelcome in both places. A well educated preacher delivers finely modulated sermons to his well-educated congregation, and the ordained high school graduate preaches to the less-educated. In short, people gravitate to their own church life as well as in social and professional life, so that Christianity preserves these social walls rather than tearing them down. This fact has been more true within Protestantism than Roman Catholicism, whose international centralization has at least furnished it a unity transcending national borders and has helped to temper regional prejudices.

The most cutting indictment against the church on this score has come from the study of American theologian H. Richard Niebuhr in his *The Social Sources of Denominationalism:*

> The division of the churches closely follows the division of men into the castes of national, racial, and economic groups. It draws the color line in the church of God; it fosters the misunderstandings, the selfexaltations, the hatreds of jingoistic nationalism by continuing in the body of Christ the spurious differences of provincial loyalties; it seats the rich and the poor apart at the table of the Lord . . .[15]

Niebuhr documented how in the history of the church the lines of earthly social prejudices, income levels, and politics have caused clashes and divisions between churches with dismaying regularity. Church groups have only rarely freed themselves from prejudices reigning in their territories. Thus in the middle 1800s northern churches were condemning slavery as wickedness, while churches of the same tradition in the south were defending it as thoroughly biblical, and denominations split on the issue. In two world wars Christians were killing one another, each side imploring God's aid in their righteous cause. In the labor struggles of past decades wealthy church groups opposed labor unions, and poor churches supported them.

These social factors even reach out to shape theological outlook, church structure, and church life. They finally get themselves so entangled with religious factors that it is hard to separate them. But nobody would doubt that they are as decisive as the purely theological factors, if not more so, in perpetuating divisions. The Baptist movement in Reformation times had a basic theological dispute in baptism with the other Protestants, but an equally powerful factor in its growth was that the Lutherans and Calvinists were strongly middle class citizens' churches, aligned with the Protestant rulers and aristocrats, whereas the Baptists spread among the lower classes who felt little affinity for and hospitality from the established churches. The Mennonites likewise found fertile field among the disinherited lower classes.

John Wesley and his friends began the Methodist movement within the Church of England as loyal Anglicans concerned for church renewal through the "method" of Bible study, preaching, and more informal meetings. But with time they felt compelled to separate themselves from the Anglican church, and it was not long before Methodist preachers found their most receptive audiences among the poor who did not feel at home in the aristocratic atmosphere of Anglicanism. These social distinctions became even more pronounced in the New World, where Anglican-Episcopalianism settled solidly in the established colonies of the eastern seaboard and the Methodists followed the rough-hewn pioneers westward with the frontier.

Many of these social factors are accidents of history which later perpetuated themselves into church divisions. The Lutherans in America are a good example. At the beginning of this century there were more than two dozen separate Lutheran groups or synods. They traced their ancestry to immigrant groups which clanned together into regional synods to preserve their home country customs, and difficulties of primitive travel made larger union unfeasible. They all considered themselves loyal Lutherans doctrinally and all shared the same sort of scattered congregationalism which American frontier conditions had made almost mandatory. In the third category, worship and piety, there were some genuine differences, largely between "high-church" and "pietist" parties, but hardly enough to justify Lutheran division.

These Lutherans were separated primarily by the social factors of coming from different countries and speaking various languages. With each new generation the process of Americanization accelerated, until now we are all Americans with only dim traces of our immigrant backgrounds. Parallel with this development was an increasing move toward merger, so that at present over 95% of American Lutheranism is concentrated into three large churches (Lutheran Church in America, Lutheran Church — Missouri Synod, and American Lutheran Church), and the rest belong to smaller groups (the Wisconsin Synod being the largest of these). Yet at the same time the few differences between these Lutheran groups have often crystallized into differences which now block further progress toward unity. Thus the American Lutheran tragedy is that what began as divisions caused largely by social and non-religious factors has now been rationalized into theological barriers standing in the way of unity.

The fact that non-religious social factors have played such a leading role in church unity and division throughout history is a dreadful shame on the church. The vision of Paul is a favorite Bible passage, but has been repeatedly an empty dream. This fact should compel all of us to take serious stock of our own church and resist the easy drift of sharing the prejudices of "our own kind," whether political, economic, social or national. We each have enough of the old Adam in us to be susceptible to the comfortable current of popular opinion, but faith constantly summons us to the sometimes uncomfortable call to follow Christ and burst the bonds of prejudices and narrow outlooks.

Since this book is dealing only with the theological and churchly causes of division, these social factors will not receive a separate chapter, though we shall bear in mind that they affect all the other three categories. But it is exceedingly important that they be mentioned, admitted, and confessed, as we consider the barriers toward unity. We shall now turn to a closer look at the first three areas of unity and division.

4.

A New Look at Doctrine

> Catholicism must endeavor to rethink Prot-
> estantism, Anglicanism and Orthodoxy . . . Prot-
> estantism, Anglicanism and Orthodoxy must do
> *the same for Catholicism and for each other.*[16]
> — Bernard Lambert, O.P.

The first decades of the Reformation carved a deep doctrinal cleavage between the Protestant reformers and the Roman Catholic church, as well as some knotty doctrinal disputes between Protestants themselves. In most instances these problems have been handed down to today's churches, and a few have been added along the way. I have already indicated how doctrinal controversies are being dealt with in ecumenical discussion (chapter 2), but there is so much yet to be done. In this chapter we shall take a closer look at what is happening in what we might call "doctrinal ecumenism."

But unless we pause and define some terms, we shall be caught in a semantic snarl from which we could never get untangled.

When we speak of "faith," we are referring to a trusting relationship with God. Of course since faith is faith "in" something, there are theological or doctrinal overtones to the word. If we speak specifically of a "Roman Catholic" faith, for example, we refer to a faith formed by Roman Catholic doctrine and church life. Every faith is nurtured and grows with some kind of doctrinal background. Yet though faith and doctrine are closely intertwined, they must not be identified. For then one would be forced to conclude that the theologian who knew the most doctrine would have the strongest faith, which Jesus flatly contradicts in speaking of the faith of little children in Matt. 18:1-4.

The word "theology" is a slippery term. Literally it means the "science of God." A basic definition might be: the attempt to articulate and explain our faith by examining the meaning of God's work of creation, redemption in Christ, and his continuing guidance by the Spirit in the church and the world. If a non-Christian asked you, "What is Christianity all about? Why do you believe?" your answer would be "theology," that is your explanation of God's works and your Christian faith.

Just as your answer would depend on your own faith and convictions as well as on the kind of person who asked the question, so the way theology is expressed depends always on the historical setting of the theologian. His language, his manner of thinking, his own religious experience, the religious problems of his neighbors, the historical situation of his country, the intellectual mentality of the times — all these factors color a man's theology. Theological expression changes with time, therefore, simply because times and circumstances change.

I shall use the term "doctrine" in its narrow sense: that which a church accepts as a statement of its belief. A doctrine can be explained in various theological ways, as long as the theological explanation remains true to the substance of the doctrine. We speak of the "doctrine of original sin," for example, yet each theologian explains this doctrine in an individual fashion. Certain doctrines are universally accepted by all Christians, such as the "doctrine of the Trinity." Churches unavoidably lay more stress on some doctrines than others. Baptists all affirm a doctrinal stand supporting adult baptism, but allow wider diversity in other matters.

Even though these three terms — faith, theology, and doctrine — are so closely interrelated, we must make distinctions to avoid a hopeless muddle. Since faith is a trusting reliance on the triune God, I can say that I am "one in faith" with fellow Christians of other churches who also trust in God. Our faiths are set in different doctrinal contexts, so that we might not define our faith identically, but in sharing a common trust in God, Christ, and the Spirit, we are "one in faith." Such a unity of faith would be questionable with those churches standing on the periphery of the Christian family (Seventh-Day Adventists, Jehovah's Witnesses, Christian Science, Unitarians, etc.), but among the churches that accept the Scriptures and stand in a historical line with the early ecumenical councils (Apostles' and Nicene Creeds), one can surely speak of a common faith.

On the other side, no one expects a uniformity of theology. Even in the New Testament, the four Gospels are distinctive because each writer has his own theological perspective and audience in mind, so each tells the same story from his own standpoint. Any given church includes various "schools of theology" and various theological ways of thinking. Theology is extremely personal and individual, and no two theologians or theologies are ever the same, though the theologians of one church all accept the doctrines of that church. Martin Luther and Philip Melanchthon, the author of the *Augsburg Confession,* were friends and co-workers for almost thirty years, but each had his own individual theological perspective. The church today needs dedicated and adventuresome theologians to meet the challenges facing Christianity, and the ecumenical movement most assuredly does not want them to be carbon copies of one another.

The problem of "doctrinal unity" is our main issue here. If we are "one in faith" with our fellow Christians, and if we cannot expect theological uniformity anyway, what do we mean by "doctrinal unity," and why should we permit doctrinal disagreements to divide us?

In considering doctrinal unity and disunity, we must begin our inquiry with these questions: Where does doctrine come from? What is the standard for judging doctrine? With this we find ourselves already in the middle of a difficult doctrinal controversy.

In rejecting many practices of the Roman Catholic church of the Middle Ages, the reformers insisted that the "Bible alone" must be the source and judge of all doctrine. This *sola scriptura* test of doctrine became a hallmark of Protestantism. The Roman Catholic bishops and theologians who assembled at Trent in the spring of 1546 discussed for over two months their response to this Reformation principle. Their answer, recognized as Roman Catholic doctrine, was this: from the teachings of Christ we have not only the "written traditions" recorded in the Bible but also the "oral traditions," never written, but passed to the church from the apostles. If we believe that Christ is present in his church and that the Spirit guides the church's doctrine, then, they concluded, we must assume that

the church's tradition down through its history has remained true. Against the Protestant *sola scriptura* the
Roman Catholic church says that Scripture and church
tradition are equally authoritative. This means that
doctrines which developed in the later history of the
church, though not explicit in the Bible (Mary's immaculate conception, for example), are proclaimed as
true and binding doctrine.

At first glance it appears that the battle lines between Protestants and Roman Catholics on this topic
are cleanly drawn. But a second look persuades us
that the issue is more complicated than that. On the
Protestant side all churches claim to take their doctrine
directly from the Scriptures, all claim to be correct
in their teachings, and all are different from one
another. Who would not have to admit there is something odd about that?

The fact of the matter is that although Protestants
claim "Scripture alone" as the source of their doctrine,
the historical tradition of each Protestant church has
been decisive in determining its doctrinal outlook.
For about 400 years Lutherans have accepted the *Book
of Concord* documents as their doctrinal statements,
that is, writings from their north German situation
which they believe accurately define biblical doctrine.
The "39 Articles" of the Anglicans and the various
catechisms of Reformed churches are all doctrinal
statements growing out of particular historical traditions and circumstances. Every Protestant church must
acknowledge that it is shaped doctrinally by its tradition, and it ought not to fall into the temptation of
imagining that its tradition is the only one striving to
be loyal to the Bible.

The irony is that a Protestant who is immovably
loyal to his church's tradition and refuses to budge

one iota from his church's inherited doctrine has surrendered the basic Protestant principle of *sola scriptura*. He has fallen victim to precisely that sin of which he accuses the Roman Catholics, namely becoming trapped in his own tradition, failing to see that biblical truth might demand a new kind of proclamation than the thought forms of past centuries. To be truly Protestant is to be not only true to one's heritage, but to allow our doctrinal concerns to be molded by the Bible's message for today's world.

A second glance at Roman Catholic thinking also complicates the picture. If one says that Scriptures and tradition have equal authority, the immediate question is: Who decides what they say? Who says which Scriptural interpretations and which traditions are doctrinally binding on Roman Catholics? The phrase of Vincent of Lerin, a monk of the 400s A.D., is the usual answer: "We hold whatever has been believed everywhere, at all times, and by everyone." In other words, a Roman Catholic believes what his church has always believed.

But the next question then arises: who determines what this is? The answer: the teaching office *(magisterium)* of the church. A Roman Catholic accepts what the church declares as the faith and doctrine of the church.

But a loose string still dangles: who is spokesman for the *magisterium?* Who decides what is official doctrine? For most of the church's history the precise answer was left ambiguous. Certain articles of faith were determined at councils and universally accepted — the person of Christ (A.D. 325, 381, 452) or the count of seven sacraments (1547). Others, such as the hierarchical-episcopal nature of the church emerged in the early centuries of church life and were subsequently accepted. But a century ago forces converged on the first Vatican Council determined to fix a final answer, which was the "infallibility" of the pope: When the pope speaks as pope *(ex cathedra,* "from the chair")* on a question of revealed doctrine or morals, his utterance is "infallible," that is, it voices without error a doctrine binding on all Roman Catholics. The *magisterium* of the Roman church is, in the end, determined by the pope.

This sounds to Protestant ears as an irrevocably final decree. But that has not turned out to be the case. The door opens to a further question: When does the pope speak infallibly? Pope Pius IX, who decreed the dogma of infallibility, had earlier issued a *Syllabus of Errors* condemning many aspects of the modern world which we now take for granted. He likely intended the *Syllabus* as an infallible decree, but the church simply did not accept it as such.

Part of the noisy discussion in Roman Catholic circles today concerning papal authority revolves around just this problem: if a pope decrees something (whether he says it is infallible or just a normal encyclical) which, it turns out, is not the opinion of the whole Roman church, has he not himself violated Vincent of Lerin's formula, and should one not say that the utterance was merely the pope's private opinion, not a binding, and surely not an infallible decree? We shall meet this problem again in the next chapter.

Despite the complexity with which the Roman Catholic church defines "Scripture and tradition" as the measure of doctrine, there has been in recent years a desire to give the Scriptures stronger consideration. To be sure, the recent Vatican Council repeats the formula of Trent:

> Therefore both sacred tradition and sacred scrip-
> ture are to be accepted and venerated with the
> same sense of devotion and reverence.[17]

But this formula was not just swallowed whole without
reflection. The "two source" notion of revelation fa-
vored by the conservatives — that truth comes from
Scripture and tradition as two quite separate streams—
was shoved aside abruptly by the council fathers. In
scholarly circles it had died a natural death for the
simple reason that there is no evidence whatsoever of
an oral, unwritten tradition which was a source of doctrine beside the Bible. The *Constitution on Revelation*
speaks rather of the intimate connection of Scripture
and tradition in the revelation of God's truth.

There is no question that Vatican II accorded the
Bible an exalted status. Apostolic preaching "is expressed in a special way in the inspired books. . . ."[18]
". . . the study of the sacred page is, as it were, the
soul of sacred theology."[19] An astounding example of
the new regard for the Bible in Roman Catholic thinking is the recent book that denies the doctrine of papal
infallibility precisely for lack of scriptural support,
written by none other than a Roman Catholic bishop.[20]

Today in ecumenical discussion a Roman Catholic
is fully as biblical as a Protestant. He would be likely
to argue, "This doctrine has been developed and formulated through centuries of tradition, but its first
beginnings and embryonic form can be seen in the
Bible." Such an idea was articulated with great force
by Cardinal John Newman a century ago. It would be
a rare Roman Catholic theologian today who would
attempt to base his doctrinal opinion on tradition
alone, with no reference whatsoever to the Scriptures,
and he would most likely be criticized most sharply
by his own colleagues.

These second glances both to the Protestant and to the Roman Catholic sides are encouraging. Protestants take "Scripture alone" as source and judge of their dogma, but they have learned to see the determinative role which their own traditions have played in their doctrines. Roman Catholics still adhere to their "Scripture and tradition" formula, but they give an increasingly important weight to the Bible.

Perhaps the crucial difference between Protestantism and the Roman Catholic view is that Protestants insist on the Bible as the final authority over tradition, rather than Trent's notion of equal authority. This means that every Protestant is committed to measure continually the teachings of his church against the ideals of Scripture. A Protestant should therefore be rethinking constantly his doctrinal convictions in view of the Bible's message to our new and changing times. He accepts his church's creeds and confessions but never sits passively on them. He is compelled to restate his doctrinal convictions in the new circumstances of today.

But are not Roman Catholic theologians striving to do exactly that same thing — to renew their theology and church life for a vital Christianity in this century? And are they not looking to the Bible as intensely as Protestants in this quest? It would be too glib to say that Protestants and Roman Catholics are about to meet suddenly in some middle ground of agreement after doing battle over "Scripture alone" versus "Scripture and tradition," with all differences miraculously disappearing. But we have found a broad ground for understanding, and we shall continue to probe the problem of Scripture and tradition together rather than against each other.

This question about the source of doctrine is just a prelude to the real doctrinal controversies that separate today's churches. But what are the long-term prospects for overcoming these divisions caused by doctrine?

We must begin by saying that doctrinal divisions are never static and unchanging. As our language and ways of thinking change over the decades, so our doctrinal perspectives change. A doctrine which might have been a source of fierce dispute when the theologians were speaking in Latin and thinking in Aristotelian categories takes on an entirely different slant when we speak English in the context of the intellectual temper of our day.

Our ecumenical task is not just to deal with the doctrinal divisions arising out of the Reformation period. Some of these problems have diminished since then, others have changed, and still others have taken on even sharper edges over the years. For example, Luther harshly criticized the worldly power and the corruption of the papacy. But today the pope is no longer a secular ruler of Rome and central Italy, and men of such caliber as Pius XII, John XXIII, and Paul VI have given the papacy a stature of unassailable piety and integrity. Yet the problem of the pope is a greater ecumenical problem today than ever during the Reformation, since papal infallibility has now been fixed as official, unchangeable dogma.

Another good example of issues that have become more difficult over the centuries is the question of Mary. The reformers rejected an overly superstitious devotion to Mary and the saints. Yet Mary's hymn of praise, the *Magnificat* in Luke 1, was one of Luther's favorite passages, and he looked on Mary as an exalted example of Christian faith. Some of his statements suggest that he personally may have believed in the lifelong virginity and even sinlessness of Mary, though he never regarded these as church dogmas. Since that time, however, Protestants have tended to label even minimal attention to Mary as "Romanism," while the Roman Catholic church has carried this devotion further, establishing it finally as dogma by decreeing the Immaculate Conception of Mary in 1854 and her Assumption into heaven in 1950. This official status of Marian devotion as dogma makes the situation much more difficult than before. Protestants have been holding their breath whether Rome will declare Mary a "coredemptrix" with Jesus, but opposition to such a term was strong enough at Vatican II to suggest that the high water mark of Marian development may have passed. The council fathers of Vatican II insisted that the topic of Mary was not a separate matter but belonged to the document on the church. Since the council there has been, and will continue to be, intense discussion on the ecumenical problem of Mary.

Lest the reader get the impression from the last two paragraphs that post-Reformation difficulties have arisen only from the Roman Catholic side, consider also this factor. In the Reformation era there were Lutherans, Calvinists, some south German reformers in between, the Anglicans in England, and a tiny minority of Baptist sects — a fairly varied crowd, but Rome could at least identify "Protestantism." But now? Not only are the Lutherans and Calvinists (Presbyterians and Reformed) splintered up all over the landscape, there is an endless array of other Protestant groups as well. In terms of sheer complexity, Protestants present a far more bewildering picture today than ever before. It is no wonder that the late Gustave

Weigel, writing on "A Catholic Looks at Protestantism," titled his first chapter "Puzzlement"! [21]

The preceding few paragraphs have shown that the
passage of time can make the ecumenical task more
difficult in certain areas, but the opposite has been
more often the case lately. The last half century has
witnessed an almost incredible advance not only in
truly understanding the doctrinal teachings of other
churches, but learning from them, and in many cases
discovering that previously assumed differences were
not so unbridgeable after all.

One of the most resounding examples of the growing understanding of earlier disputes occurred in 1957
with the publication of a book by the Swiss-born Roman Catholic scholar Hans Küng, entitled *Justification.*
The doctrine of justification stands at the heart of the
Reformation faith, the article of faith "on which the
church stands or falls." No single issue occupied more
theological energy in the 16th century than this key
doctrine of "justification by grace through faith,"
which has been a banner of Protestantism ever since.
One of the staunchest defenders of this evangelical
heritage in this century was the late Reformed theologian Karl Barth.

Father Küng studied the works of Barth carefully and
came to this conclusion: There is nothing in Barth's
doctrine of justification which contradicts the Roman
Catholic view. Barth himself wrote at the beginning of
this book:

> *All I can say is this: If what you have presented in
> Part Two of this book is actually the teaching of
> the Roman Catholic Church, then I must certainly
> admit that my view of justification agrees with the
> Roman Catholic view.*[22]

Küng's exposition of the doctrine has meanwhile never been rejected by Roman authorities.

What has happened is this: Four hundred years make an enormous difference in the lines of controversy. Tempers have long since cooled, bristling polemics often based on caricatured misunderstandings have given way to objective study and fraternal dialog, our languages are different, and the whole setting of the problem has changed.

Fr. Küng's judgment does not of course apply in all aspects to Lutheran theology or other non-Barthian Protestants. But it hits closely enough to make the point clear. A Roman Catholic today holds to "justification by grace through faith" as much as an evangelical Protestant. "I doubt if it would be possible today to develop a first-class debate with mutually exclusive positions between Roman and non-Roman leaders of thought on this subject," wrote the late Douglas Horton.[23] There are of course still differences in our interpretations which not even Fr. Küng or Mr. Horton claimed had vanished. Our understanding of grace and faith, the role of indulgences, and other problems occupy us still. But the passage of time modifies doctrinal problems, so that we must always reassess the changing patterns of doctrinal outlook.

Another area of progress toward doctrinal understanding is the current rethinking on the sacraments. No area of doctrine has been a more bitterly disputed territory than this topic. The Lord's Supper, intended as a "sacrament of unity," has become the most persistent and stubborn sign of our disunity. Ecumenical groups discuss, eat, pray, sing, and worship together, but only the daring *avant-garde* (usually the young, who are less inhibited by church regulations) will venture to celebrate Communion across denominational lines. Ironically, baptism has become a genuine sacrament of unity, since practically all churches accept the valid baptism of other churches, except of course those who reject infant baptism. Vatican II declared: "Baptism, therefore, constitutes a sacramental bond of unity linking all who have been reborn by means of it." [24]

Much of the debate over the sacraments between Protestants and Roman Catholics has resembled two boxers flailing away wildly and seldom hitting anything. I remember well an evening when the young people of our congregation met with the youth of the neighboring Roman Catholic parish. The priest and I had agreed to stay out of the discussion for fear of dominating the conversation. We were to be experts on the sidelines, which meant drinking coffee in the kitchen. Later we learned that in one group a Roman Catholic youth had stated that he believed in seven sacraments, but could not remember what they all were. In another group two of my young people argued between themselves whether Protestants had three or four sacraments. (Was it poor memory on their part or an indictment of weak confirmation instruction on mine?!)

One factor has given the discussion on the sacraments new life: understanding that the word "sacrament" is not in the Bible at all. *Sacramentum* first makes its appearance in the Latin translation of the New Testament, where the Greek word for "mystery" (in the singular) is translated fifteen times as *mysterium* and eight times as *sacramentum,* with little rhyme or reason why one then the other. The Latin word *sacramentum* meant an oath of allegiance or a financial deposit made in a courtroom. Why it was used for "mystery" is literally a mystery to us. Our English translations have wisely returned to the original sense and used "mystery" in all passages (or "secret" in the New English Bible).

The word "sacrament" did not enter popular usage until later than four centuries after Christ, by the time the Latin Bible had become the accepted version. Then it came to be understood as a sign or symbol of a hidden mystery. St. Augustine spoke of a sacrament as a visible sign of something invisible. The scholastic theologians developed the thought at great length. The number was set at seven—baptism, Eucharist, confirmation, penance, marriage, ordination, and extreme unction. In addition, the Roman church also spoke of "sacramentals," those rites and prayers instituted by the church, such as consecrations, benedictions, sign of the cross, holy water, rosary, and others.

The Reformation rejected this broad concept of sacraments and specified as sacraments only those acts which Christ instituted, in which God is present with his Word through visible elements, offering forgiveness of sins. This brought the number to two, baptism and the Lord's Supper, although some early Reformers also included penance, considering the spoken word of forgiveness as a visible means of grace.

"How many" sacraments is of course an obvious point of contention. Protestants count only two, although with the exception of extreme unction (the anointing of the sick and dying) they include all the Roman sacraments in their church rites without labeling them sacraments. But more basic than the number of sacraments are the questions: what *is* a sacrament, and what is the place of the sacraments in the church's life?

Since the word "sacrament" is not in the Bible, we

can for a moment declare a moratorium on our quarrels over the term itself and examine together what the New Testament intends to say with the original word *mysterion.* This Greek word originally expressed the feeling of those people that the capricious ways of the gods were part of the unknown and dreaded fate of man. Into this atmosphere came the Christian gospel declaring that the mystery of God has now been revealed in his Son, Jesus Christ. If we look carefully, we see that in those New Testament instances where *mysterion* was translated *sacramentum,* it usually implies the mystery now revealed in Christ.

> For he has made known to us in all wisdom and insight the mystery *(sacramentum)* of his will, according to his purpose which he set forth in Christ . . . (Eph. 1:9)
> . . . the mystery *(sacramentum)* was made known to me by revelation . . . (Eph. 3:3)
> . . . the unsearchable riches of Christ, and to make all men see what is the plan of the mystery *(sacramentum)* hidden for ages in God . . . (Eph. 3:8-9)
> . . . the glory of this mystery *(sacramentum)* which is Christ in you. (Col. 1:27)

So to be true to the New Testament, the *sacramentum,* or God's revealed mystery, is above all Christ himself. To use the language of the early church, Christ himself is the most profound visible sign of God's invisible grace.

What has actually happened in ecumenical discussion is that instead of talking about this or that sacrament, we speak first of Christ as *the* sacrament, the visible revelation of God's mystery. The book, *Christ the Sacrament,* by Fr. Edward Schillebeeckx, a leading Dutch theologian, is an example of this line of thinking. Many speak also of the "sacrament of the church," since the church conveys Christ and the gospel. Even the term "sacrament of the world," used to express God's grace in his creation, is heard. Both phrases indicate the attention which the concept of mystery-sacrament is receiving today.

The whole question of sacraments appears now in an entirely new light. A century ago we were hung up on the problem: is it a sacrament or not? Now we begin with the primary sacrament, Jesus Christ, and ask how all these other rites we call "sacraments" are related to him. Until now we were preoccupied with the specific question: in what way was this or that rite instituted or commanded by Christ? Now this and other similar questions are considered in the light of their meaning in relation to Christ himself. Which rites we actually call sacraments is subordinate to the real issue of how they are "sacraments" in terms of conveying Christ, the true sacrament.

In short, on the question of sacraments we have a virtually new approach, or at least a much more fruitful and hopeful one. This simple shift of emphasis carries with itself vast implications. For example, the *number* of sacraments is no longer such an overwhelming topic. A study by a French priest, "Why Are There Seven Sacraments?" concludes:

> The proposition "There are seven sacraments" means that there is only one (since seven is a symbol for totality)—and that in this one everything can be turned to sacrament: Christ, the tangible sign of the Mystery of love of the God who adopts men as his sons.[25]

He criticizes the "closed, arithmetical, and legalistic notion of seven sacraments 'neither more nor less.' " Whether one agrees with his argument or not, it is clear that fresh winds are blowing within this whole topic.

Today's ecumenical study of the sacraments suggests some exciting possibilities. Might it not be possible, for instance, for all Christians to acknowledge a unique and special sacramental role of the two sacraments, baptism and the Lord's Supper, in the life of the church? Every Christian receives them, unlike marriage and ordination. They are generally acts of the assembled Christian community, unlike anointing the sick. And they are rooted unquestionably in the New Testament, unlike confirmation, whose historical roots are shaky. Fr. Yves Congar, the French Dominican who deserves special tribute as an ecumenical pioneer when ecumenism was unpopular, published an article on "The Idea of 'Major' or 'Principle' Sacraments," in which he argues:

> The idea that some sacraments are more important than others, particularly baptism and the Eucharist, is well supported by traditional theology.[26]

He points to St. Thomas Aquinas, who also referred to baptism and the Eucharist as "the principle sacraments." Even the pointedly anti-Protestant Council of Trent refused to say that all seven sacraments were equal in every sense. Fr. Congar considers these the "major" sacraments because they were both instituted by Christ and are central in the church's life. He is not of course suddenly becoming "Protestant," for he considers the other five an essential part of the church's sacramental character, each in its own distinctive way. Yet his suggestion offers fascinating opportunities for ecumenical dialog.

This turns the challenge to the Protestant side. It should be possible for Protestants to use the word "sacrament" in its wider New Testament sense, related to the revealed mystery in Christ. Even though Protestants would not likely add more sacraments to their two, it should not be impossible to use the adjective "sacramental" more flexibly. Most Protestants give confirmation "sacramental" meaning without thinking, simply because they explain its meaning in connection with baptism. Ordination has sacramental significance if for no other reason than men are commissioned through ordination to administer the sacraments. Few would deny marriage sacramental meaning, since it was established by God in creation and sanctified by Christ himself. This line of thinking can enrich Protestant thinking.

It would be wholly naive to say that the ecumenical question of the sacraments is practically solved. There are plenty of difficult questions still ahead of us. But this short excursion should make it clear to the reader how careful biblical study and earnest dialog can lead to closer understanding and mutual benefit on such problems. These theological efforts on all sides have led to what surely can be called a breakthrough in this question, until now one of the greatest doctrinal causes of separation.

Progress will continue among churches toward understanding of doctrinal matters such as justification, the sacraments, and others. Most likely some doctrinal issues which once divided churches will be eliminated as divisive barriers. But growing doctrinal accord and consensus is only part of the issue. A more basic question is: why do we permit doctrines to divide us anyway? Or, on which doctrinal questions must there be agreement for a united church, and on which can there be disagreement without divisions?

These are intricately complex questions, but we

should understand what is involved. There are really two sides to these questions—the variety of doctrine allowed in a church, and the variety of ways a doctrine can be expressed.

First, every church has some degree of doctrinal flexibility. We think of Roman Catholicism as a church with a whole edifice of dogma, but its "official" doctrinal statements are relatively few. For example, the Roman Catholic Church has no one "doctrine" of Christ's atonement. Throughout church history one finds many views of Christ's work, but none has been established as *the* dogma. One speaks about the "Roman Catholic doctrine of the church," but such a doctrine embraces a wide spectrum of ideas, and the emphasis from one view to another can shift with time, as it in fact has done. There is a broad consensus on such a doctrine, but in its detail it is not at all fixed.

Every church claims some definitive doctrinal stands, but these dogmas do not cover nearly all matters of faith. In any church therefore one finds a wide variety of doctrinal and theological outlooks which might cause disagreement but not divisions. Such variety exists within the unity of that church.

One can hardly speak of a requirement for total doctrinal unity in the New Testament church. The simple creed "Jesus is Lord" appears to be the only doctrinal standard of those first years. The cross and resurrection were articles of faith, not doctrines, and each of the New Testament writers described these events and their meaning in his own way. This was before the day of confessions and dogmas, when the common faith of these scattered and often harrassed Christians held them together.

But creeds and doctrines became necessary as heretical opinions arose and struck at the heart of the

Christian faith. From these early struggles we have the three ancient creeds—Apostles', Nicene, Athanasian. Other doctrinal disputes produced more dogmas through the years, yet until the time of the Reformation very few statements could be called rigidly fixed doctrines. But since the 1500s churches have splintered into tiny groups over various doctrinal squabbles.

On closer look one sees that a church lays great weight on those doctrines it considers central and allows diversity on others. The Lutherans, for example, insist on a consensus on their doctrine of the Lord's Supper for unity or fellowship, but not on any one doctrine of the ministry. Yet Anglicans have very nearly the opposite point of view.

Most churchmen would agree that for unity agreement only on essential matters of doctrine is necessary. This is the opinion of the *Augsburg Confession*, as we have seen, ". . . agree concerning the teaching of the gospel and the administration of the sacraments." But Lutherans have not been able to agree on how much or how little this includes. In the documents of Vatican II even the Roman Catholics recognize a "hierarchy of truths,"[27] suggesting that some matters are more central than others. But no attempt was made at the Vatican Council to specify which doctrinal truths stood at the peak of this hierarchy, and had such an attempt at definition been made, there would surely have been wide ranging dissension.

So in back of the discussion on various dogmas stands the basic question of how much doctrinal agreement is required for unity. The second aspect of this background question deals with varying interpretations of the same doctrine. Two theologians could be loyal to the same doctrinal heritage yet might offer differing, even clashing interpretations. We come back to the definitions at the beginning of the chapter. Dogmas are brief statements of a church's abiding convictions. But they must be explained theologically, and theologians or theologies are too closely tied to their times and circumstances for a church to decree any one as official or permanent. The Athanasian creed is a statement of our belief, but with its ancient language and thought pattern it is monotonous gibberish for many of us. Its thought and intent must be explained anew. Two scholars might accept the creed but not be wholly pleased with the interpretations given by each other.

A good example of this occurred in the 1963 world assembly of the Lutheran World Federation in Helsinki, Finland. Lutheran theologians who accepted their church's doctrine of justification had difficulty reaching agreement on a modern formulation of this doctrine. Journalists had a field day, claiming that Lutherans were no longer unanimous on the central article of their faith. The fact is, they were unanimous in their adherence to the doctrine but were unwilling to have any one contemporary exposition of the doctrine elevated to a semi-official status.

Roman Catholics are currently rethinking church dogmas. Twenty years ago most people assumed that Roman dogma was synonymous with scholastic theology, but this is not true today. In one of his most celebrated statements Pope John XXIII liberated Roman theologians to renew their theological expression into relevance for the modern world when he distinguished between the constant deposit of faith and the changing needs of theology in his opening address to the second Vatican Council:

The substance of the ancient doctrine of the de-

positium fidei is one thing; the way in which it is
expressed is another.[28]

One example of this rethinking is the discussion in
Roman Catholic circles on what explanation can accurately convey the meaning of the doctrine of "transubstantiation." This term was serviceable when everyone thought in Aristotelian forms, but it makes little
sense today. Even among theologians who accept the
dogma there is disagreement on what English language
terms best correspond to the original intent of the
idea.

It is extremely difficult and risky for a church body
to arbitrate between theological interpretations. "Conservatives" often cling protectively to the familiar, perhaps outmoded, way of expression with little willing-
ness to meet any new dogmatic problems. "Liberals"
sometimes embrace every novel theological fad which
raises its head, cutting themselves off from the vast
majority of believers who have not read the latest
theological hit off the press. The best judge of such
things is usually the passage of time itself. New interpretations which genuinely meet the needs of church
life will endure and overshadow formulations whose
time has passed. Theological fads will die out, or at
least shrink to their proper perspectives.

But for ecumenical discussions today and in years
to come, this problem of various doctrinal interpretations persists. Two churches might agree on the dogma
of original sin, but theologians within each church
would describe it in various ways. Can one, then,
speak of a united doctrinal view within or between
these churches? Probably yes, since the church groups
and theologians claim loyalty to their inherited doctrines — and we must after all trust in each other's

ntegrity — but it would be quite impossible and undesirable to pose any one contemporary theological position as *the* accepted stance of the church today.

Doctrine has been and will remain a major source of church division. We shall overcome many of these divisions as misunderstandings are cleared away and as perspectives change with time. But how much doctrinal agreement is necessary for unity or fellowship? This question will become even more pressing in the future. For church union there must be a solid base of doctrinal accord to avoid a hodge-podge of conflicting ideas on basic issues. But where does one draw the line between such unanimity on essential matters and an unattainable and unbiblical uniformity on all topics?

Particularly those of us in churches which have strong doctrinal traditions must continually reexamine what we mean by "doctrinal unity." Of course we believe in the truth of our church's doctrines, but to see truth neatly tied and packaged within the confines of our own opinions is a bit presumptuous. We find ourselves in the middle, endeavoring to be loyal to the truth but knowing that truth transcends our views, for

now we see in a mirror dimly, but then face to face (1 Cor. 13:12).

5.

Ministry and Structure

"The greatest hang-up in the church"
— America Magazine

The title of this chapter covers a wide terrain indeed. Here we confront problems that lie at the heart of every conversation which relates to church union or merger, problems that often prove more difficult to overcome than doctrinal issues.

We begin with the problem of structure, and in sketching the three basic forms of church structure we shall provide a skeleton for some other questions in this chapter. A church body can fall into one of three patterns:

1) The *hierarchical form* has a clear line of authority from the top to the bottom. Clergymen and congregations are subject to somebody above them who is called a bishop, superintendent, or some other name. Within a few centuries after Christ, the whole Christian church fit into this pattern. The Roman Catholic church is the most obvious example today, but Anglicans and Orthodox also have this form.

2) Reformation leaders sought to return to the church structures of the New Testament church, though the Bible is vague about such matters, as we

shall soon see. One result was the *presbyterian form* of structure. A presbytery is a group of elders, pastors and laymen, representing congregations of a certain area and administering the affairs of these parishes. Below the presbytery are the councils in each congregation called "sessions," and above the presbyteries is an assembly of representatives from all presbyteries. But the basic ruling body is the presbytery. This system comes from John Calvin's Reformed church in Geneva and is characteristic of Reformed and Presbyterian churches throughout the world.

3) The *congregational form* sees in the New Testament church an example of decentralized congregations united more by their common faith than by super-organizations. This type gives the individual congregation broad sovereignty, such as determining its own pastor, program, and finances. A synodical organization above the congregation is more advisory and coordinating than authoritative and exists specially for those projects too large for single parishes to manage such as missions, schools, and charitable works. This structure found fertile soil among Protestant "free churches," especially in England and America. The Congregationalists took the description as their name, but the Baptists represent the largest group of congregationalist churches. Almost all Pentecostals belong here. Lutherans in the United States are basically congregationalist, in direct contrast to hierarchical European Lutheranism.

Each type has obvious advantages and disadvantages. The hierarchical system is streamlined and efficient, but since authority and responsibility are focused on the top, the people on the bottom rung may become apathetic or resentful. Since the congregational system centers authority in the congregations with little centralized authority above the parish, the larger church's efforts toward a given goal may be sporadic and uncoordinated. The presbyterian system has often been characterized as "bishop-by-committee" and has the advantages of broader participation, but also the drawbacks of sometimes sluggish committee operation.

Of course there is no absolutely "pure" example of any one of these types anywhere in the world. Nearly every church has incorporated elements of two or all of these basic forms. But despite such overlapping, they do depict three distinct patterns, and this pattern emerges when one observes the church in operation. When the dust finally settles, who has the final say in the decisions — the bishop, representatives of a group of congregations, or the single congregation?

If any reader thinks these forms are only theoretical, a series of practical questions will serve to help him place his own church in this spectrum and will illustrate how these "theoretical" differences affect every aspect of a church's daily life.

What can your pastor do that a layman cannot? Hierarchical churches connect the idea of the ministry to the office of the bishop and his authority to ordain and thus give the priest or pastor a very distinctive role. In the Roman Catholic church only a priest can consecrate bread and wine in the mass and hear confessions, that is, administer the sacraments. Exceptions are made only in rare cases of emergency. In Presbyterian churches a layman ordained as an elder has a high station, sharing many duties with the pastor (who is also counted as an ordained elder). In most Baptist and Pentecostal churches ordination is not considered an exalted status, and a layman is often called on to preside over the worship service. Methodists, though hierarchical in structure, have a strong tradition of lay pastors. Lutherans are in the middle. They have no detailed doctrine of the ministry, but for the sake of order they agree that no one should perform ministerial functions without a regular call and ordination. Nevertheless, there have been instances of lay movements in Lutheran history, such as the followers of Hans Nielson Hauge in Norway.

Who determines who your pastor will be? In a hierarchical church the bishop, superintendent, or overseer appoints him. In presbyterian churches he is called by the presbytery. In congregationalist churches, the congregation itself selects and calls its pastor, with or without advice from any district or synodical official. But here again we find a good deal of overlapping. A bishop or a presbytery would seldom make such a decision without consulting the congregation and might likely accept the parish's own choice. Since American Lutherans are basically congregationalist, the right of calling the pastor belongs to the parish, but the clear trend is that parishes rely increasingly on the suggestions of their district presidents. It would be in fact ticklish business for a parish to call a man without the district president's approval.

Who has authority over your pastor? In hierarchical groups he can operate independently of the congregation, since he is under the bishop. In congregationalist churches he works together with the council of his congregation with only loose ties to synodical oversight. Among the Reformed churches, the presbyteries hold such authority.

What authority does the council of your congregation really have?

Who determines and administers the financial affairs of your congregation? Who owns the property, for example, and who decides such things as building a new church? In hierarchical forms the clergy generally control the purse strings. Among congregationalists the lay members of the parish have the majority decision.

Could your congregation leave its synod or church body if it so desired?

Who selects the higher officials of your church — bishop, district president, church president? In the Roman Catholic church only the cardinals elect the pope, and only the pope in turn names cardinals and bishops. In presbyterian and congregationalist systems such elections are by vote, and laymen carry as much weight in the balloting as the clergy.

Such questions could go on, but if the reader reflects on these, he will see that this matter of ministry and structure is indeed a tremendously critical area. It is no wonder that merger plans get snarled more often here than on doctrinal questions!

With this basic frame of reference in mind, we ask ourselves, "What then does the Bible advise in matters of ministry and structure?" Above all we see that the New Testament does not set out any pre-conceived notion of ministry, structure, and authority. One gets the impression from these early writings that the apostles had a job to do and that they organized their work and their churches in order to accomplish it as best they could. It is also clear that the original apostles and Paul exercised a special ministry and authority simply because they were co-workers of Jesus, or in Paul's case because he was especially called. Peter was likely recognized as the natural leader among the apostles since he usually seized the initiative among the disciples and since Jesus addressed him specifically several times.[30] But there is no biblical evidence that he had any specific authority over the others. At the Jerusalem Council of the early church, Paul's opinion prevailed over Peter's (Acts 15; Gal. 2). It is possible that Peter assumed the leadership of the church in Rome as its "bishop," but we cannot determine this from the pages of the New Testament.

Paul took for granted that his authority enabled him to arbitrate controversies, pass judgment, and issue orders.[31] He also took it on himself to send men into congregations (Tychicus, Timothy, and Titus). Peter, James, and John apparently were the leaders of the first congregation in Jerusalem.

It was of course necessary for individual congregations to have their own leaders. The first record we have of congregational officials is the office of the "deacons" in the Jerusalem church. The founding of this office deserves a close look. The group of Christians was growing, and "the twelve" could no longer do all the administration themselves. So to devote their time to preaching, they held a congregational meeting and told the people to "pick out from among you seven men of good repute, full of the Spirit and of wisdom, whom we may appoint to this duty," namely charity work (Acts 6).

This passage is interesting, first because the process of naming deacons was obviously democratic, but secondly because after their election they were "appointed" and consecrated into their office by the disciples. In a discussion concerning authority in today's church this becomes a favorite passage for those urging more democracy and congregational responsibility. But it also includes an apostolic office (or bishop) who somehow confirms or ratifies the action of the people. The whole episode indicates how impossible it is to categorize the early church into any single pattern or structure.

More important is the position of the "elders" (Greek *presbyteros,* source of our word "presbyter"). It was taken from the Jewish office of "elder," and we cannot determine the extent of his authority from the Scriptures. This office first appears in Acts 11:30, where Paul and Barnabas "appointed elders for them in every church." The verb "appoint" here means literally "to choose by a show of hands," but it is not necessarily limited to that meaning, so we cannot draw certain conclusions about the method of selection. But it seems apparent that in any given town or church there were a number of elders in charge of the congregation. They were the clergy of the early church. (The terms "priest" and "pastor" were not used in the New Testament church. They came later.)

The whole picture becomes a bit more complicated with the addition of the title "bishop" (Greek *episcopos,* source of our word "episcopal"). Scholars agree that the term "elder" and "bishop" were originally used interchangeably in the New Testament church. The term *presbyteros* was taken from current Jewish usage and *episcopos* was its non-Jewish Greek equivalent, meaning "overseer" or "guardian." This certainly appears to be the case in Acts 20, where Luke mentions the "elders" *(presbyteroi)* of Ephesus, whom Paul then addresses as "guardians," *(episcopoi*—Acts 20:17, 28). When Paul greets the "bishops and deacons" of Philippi, he obviously means the elders and deacons (Phil. 1:1). Paul also speaks of bishops as if they were shepherds (Acts 20:28), the same metaphor Peter ascribes to the elders (1 Peter 2:25, 5:1-4).

Very soon, however, the word "bishop" appears in the singular, implying that in a community there would be one bishop among many elders. Paul, for example, outlines the duties of various offices and writes about "a bishop . . . the office of a bishop" in the singular, then about "deacons" and "elders" in the plural.[32] We can only suppose that the title of bishop was gradually given to the senior elder (or perhaps to the elder celebrating the Eucharist at the time), who then became the chairman of the elders.

From there it was a logical step for a bishop to be the leader of several smaller congregations within an area, each of which was served directly by elders. This process occurred sooner in some places than in others. St. Ignatius, bishop of Antioch less than a century after Pentecost, urged obedience to the bishop as a guarantee of the church's unity under persecution. During the course of the second century, the office of the bishop as head over one or more congregations became universal. He was, however, probably elected by the congregation along with the elders and deacons, and it may not have been a lifetime position. Toward the end of the first century Clement, an elder of Rome, wrote that the bishops continued the ministry of those preceding, but a doctrine that the bishops were the direct successors of the twelve apostles was not articulated until centuries later.

Each congregation or community seemed to be relatively autonomous. Nevertheless, it was inevitable that certain churches would emerge with special distinction and prestige, particularly those in which apostles had worked, or those in the great metropolitan centers. Jerusalem was obviously the first important focal point, having been the scene of Jesus' passion, the site of Pentecost and the original "home church" of Christendom. Antioch soon became a key church, since it was the missionary headquarters of Paul and according to legend also a church in which Peter worked. As the church spread across the Mediterranean, it was inevitable that it would point toward the heart of the empire, the "eternal city" of Rome, where Christianity was officially recognized in A.D. 313. The great African center of learning and culture, Alexandria in Egypt, became the focus of African Christianity. Finally, the church found root in Constantinople (today Istanbul), the eastern axis of the empire.

The bishops of these five great centers came to be known as the "patriarch" bishops of the church. At first they had no special authority over the other bishops in their regions, except for the prestige of their own dioceses, but slowly they assumed more jurisdiction over their areas. Yet the patriarchs recognized each other as equals.

This was the situation after about the first 500 years of the church's existence. By the end of the next 500 years it was quite different. First, the rise of Mohammedanism swept Asia and Africa, obliterating Jerusalem, Antioch, and Alexandria as major Christian centers. That left Rome and Constantinople, the western and eastern poles of the Roman empire, each with its own way of thinking. After centuries of bickering they finally excommunicated each other in 1054, dividing Christendom into the Orthodox church of the East and the Roman church of the West. The Orthodox churches retained at least nominal patriarchs and metropolitan bishops of the ancient dioceses, so that even though the bishop of Constantinople was granted the respect of the leading bishop, the other important bishops retained equal authority. But since the Western church was left with only one of the original patriarchs, the development of the Roman bishopric into a centralized papacy became virtually a foregone conclusion in the West.

After this breathlessly short excursion into early church history, what have we learned? We learned that Christ did not dictate any detailed pattern of ministry, structure, or authority to his church. He gave them the mission of Matthew 28 — making disciples, baptizing, and teaching. From this grew the ministry of preaching, teaching, leading worship, and administering sacraments. In time much of this was done by men specially trained, selected, and consecrated for the task — thus we have the clergy. For the work of charity it became necessary to appoint men for this job — hence the deacons. To any community leaders are necessary — so elders and bishops also became part of the Christian congregation.

But one cannot read the New Testament with the impression "this is how our setup *has* to be," since there is no fixed doctrine of ministry and authority in those books. John McKenzie, Roman Catholic professor at Notre Dame, notes:

> The impression which the early church leaves of itself is that it was very tolerant of variation in form and function; there is no clear deliberate effort to reach fixity of structure. The office and function can be modified to meet existing situations.[33]

When American Roman Catholic and Lutheran scholars met in late 1968 to discuss this matter, they concluded that it is "evident that there was no demonstrable normative pattern of the ministry during the period covered by the New Testament."

Since the Bible does not dictate any one pattern of ministry or structure, and since each basic structure can find elements of support within Scripture, another interesting possibility for tomorrow's church comes to mind. Why not combine the best aspects of each system into one church structure — take a little here, give a little there, and stir it all together? This is not as preposterous as it sounds. Stephen Rose, one of America's most persistent critics of today's complacent churches, has such a vision:

> My preference is for a Presbyterian polity with bishops playing a role somewhat similar to that of today's Episcopal bishops. The relative autonomy of cooperative ministeries would tend to satisfy those who see the positive merits of the free church tradition.[34]

This may indeed be the shape of the church tomorrow, but it will not happen by tossing the ingredients into a pot, stirring vigorously, and making a stew. Mergers and church unions ought not to be, and are not, horse-trading sessions where men put together a patchwork compromise to make everybody happy. Rather we must realize — and here is the key lesson of the New Testament regarding structure — that the church has a mission, a job to do, and the kind of ministry, organization, and structure it assumes is *for the sake of this mission*. Every church, whether involved in a merger or not, must continually ask, "What is the best structure for doing our work?"

This is why Eugene Carson Blake, general secretary of the World Council of Churches, dismisses a method of mere compromise:

> We are convinced that we will get nowhere by a compromise procedure, for example, "You Anglicans can have bishops, but we Congregationalists will balance that by retaining absolute independen-

cy of the congregations, and we will let the Presbyterians have their ruling elders." [35]

It was Mr. Blake who first proposed the union of Presbyterian, Episcopal, Methodist, and Congregational
churches in a 1960 sermon. His plan was for "a united
church, truly catholic, truly reformed, and truly evangelical." But rather than a grand mixture, he hoped for
a thorough study of structure, so that these groups
now working in the Consultation on Church Union
(COCU) might adopt an organizational form best
suited for carrying out the mission of the church. It
would of course involve combining elements from
the various church groups, but for the sake of service,
not compromise — an important difference!

The formation of the Church of South India in 1947
was a milestone in the ecumenical movement because
it brought together Methodists, Presbyterians, Congregationalists, and five Anglican dioceses. Here, too,
it was accomplished through an intensive study of the
nature and mission of the church, which was particularly urgent since this church feels a strong mission
call in a non-Christian country. One of the key results
of this study was that this church became "episcopal,"
that is, it retained the office of bishop. In doing so it
devoted a great deal of fruitful thinking on what a
bishop should be.

The question of bishops will continue to be a central
issue in the ecumenical movement. This is particularly
true of Lutherans, since American Lutherans have no
bishops and most European Lutherans do. A worldwide
study was recently completed by the Lutheran World
Federation on just this question, entitled *Episcopacy in
the Lutheran Church?*

To clear the issue a bit, let us not make the mistake

of getting bogged down in titles. To quibble whether a church official should be called a "bishop" or "district president" should not arouse much excitement these days. Almost every Protestant church in existence has men roughly equivalent to bishops, even if they avoid the title like poison. An English free church pastor jumps over most of the pro and con arguments about bishops by stating the obvious:

> The free churches are already episcopal. If episcopacy is rightly derived from *episcope* and has reference to the oversight or shepherding of the church, especially in a sphere wider than the local congregations, it must be said that all the English free churches have developed organs for this purpose ... Methodists call them Chairmen, Congregationalists (not very felicitously) Moderators, Baptists, Superintendents.[36]

Mr. Mayor adds that these positions might not have the authority of a Roman Catholic or Anglican bishop, but their function is bishopric in nature.

So if everybody changed all these names to "bishop," would the ecumenical problem be solved? Of course not. The question is not one of titles. Actually we are not even asking, "Should we have bishops?", since every church has some kind of position of oversight, whatever the title. The real question is: What is the nature, function, and authority of this office of bishop, district president, or chairman? (We can assume, I think, that united churches of the future will consistently adopt the title of bishop, simply because it is so deeply rooted in church history and has been retained by the vast majority of Christian churches throughout history. It is just a better title than any other.)

This question of the nature of church leadership is being studied intensely not only between churches, but within every church. In the Roman Catholic church the role of the bishop has become an enormously critical issue. In American Lutheran churches we discuss the role of the church or district presidents — different titles but the same issue. As in all questions of ministry and structure, we make our inquiry from the standpoint of the church's mission: what should a bishop or president be if the church is to serve as well as it can today?

Most of the present discussion gravitates to the problem of authority. We live in an anti-authoritarian age. This reflects itself in a healthy skepticism for church authority, which in the past has been as heavy-handed as any secular authority. Lutherans have unfortunately contributed little to the discussion, perhaps because they cannot make up their own minds about questions concerning structure.

The most penetrating and creative thinking on this matter is coming from Roman Catholic scholars. This is perhaps inevitable, since so much authority has accumulated in the Roman hierarchy. One of the best examples of this research is the book by Fr. Mc-Kenzie already mentioned, *Authority in the Church*. His introduction states the heart of the problem, "The Nature of Authority," in which he examines "how church authority differs from other forms of authority." [37] His study of the New Testament leads him to insist that "the transformation of the church into a power structure is ... a perversion of authority." [38] The true biblical and Christian concept of authority is a leadership of service, love, and discipleship in Christ and the Spirit, a radical departure from much church practice. A bishop or president is in no sense a "boss," whose subjects submit to him, but a pastoral leader. Whether this ideal is attainable, only time will tell, but it is the proper ideal.

For a Roman Catholic, and for anyone engaged in ecumenical discussions with Roman Catholics, the question of authority concerns not only the local bishops but focuses finally upon the authority of the bishop of Rome, the pope, the supreme authority in the Roman church. Here we come to one of the most imposing obstacles on the path to Christian unity. Pope Paul VI realizes this as well as anyone, as he addressed the members of his Secretariat for Christian Unity: "The pope, as we well know, is undoubtedly the gravest obstacle in the path of ecumenism." [39] The papacy presents a two-fold problem. First, the pope claims supreme authority in the structure and governing of the church as the one "vicar of Christ" on earth. The second formidable obstacle is the pope's infallibility, his claim to speak on behalf of the Holy Spirit without human error on matters of revealed doctrine and morals. For a Protestant it is unthinkable that any human being could equate his words with the Word of the Spirit as incapable of human mistakes.

The problem of papal infallibility is difficult. With one side saying "yes" and the other "no," there appears to be no ground or room for discussion.

> The problem remains unresolvable in any humanly foreseeable way, for . . . there is no halfway house between accepting and rejecting infallibility, no such thing as "being a little bit infallible." [40]

But Mr. Brown then adds, "Yet the impasse is not as total as once appeared. . . ." The pope's authority and his infallibility are subjects of searching reexamination among Roman Catholic scholars. Especially younger

Roman Catholic theologians reject the idea of the pope as some kind of monarch with absolute power. They visualize instead a pope who symbolizes the unity of the church, whose leadership is inspirational and fatherly rather than dictatorial, and who speaks with authority only when and because he truly expresses the mind of the whole church.

To counterbalance the one-sided idea of individual "infallibility," Vatican II employed the term "collegiality." The pope governs the church and speaks infallibly in union with the "college of bishops." For a growing number of Roman thinkers this word "collegiality" means that the pope does not have an isolated monarchical authority of his own apart from the consensus of the bishops, even though all bishops recognize him as their head, spokesman, and shepherd. American Roman Catholic writer John Sheerin describes the effect of this doctrine:

> Now the old concept of the Pope as oriental potentate could give way to the concept of the apostolic college, a group of bishops caring for and supervising the flock of Christ as the small flock at Jerusalem was supervised by the college, with Peter as chief shepherd.[41]

It was in this spirit that the bishops assembled at the Bishops' Synod at Rome in the fall of 1969 and so strongly urged the pope to consult them before making any important pronouncements.

Indeed, the main reason for the explosive reaction against the 1968 birth control encyclical *Humanae Vitae* was that Pope Paul acted "uncollegially," making the declaration against the will of large numbers of Roman Catholic laymen, clergy, and bishops, including even the majority of his own birth control advisory commission. Yet in fairness to Pope Paul one must add that his overall vision of papal leadership is not out of harmony with contemporary thinking. At a general audience in 1967 he reminded his listeners that Jesus' last encounter with Peter was the command to "feed my sheep," and Pope Paul concluded:

> Peter's primacy of leadership and service for the Christian people should be a pastoral primacy, a primacy of love.[42]

The problem of the papacy might seem unsolvable now, but it is surely premature to assume that the situation will remain unchanged. Roman theologians will continue to study these issues of ministry, authority, and infallibility in years to come, and there will certainly be a steady development of outlook.

In a sense the Roman Catholics are throwing the ball back to the Protestants. They have displayed an openness to probe honestly and critically into these problems. What was once a tiny avant-garde hoping for change has swelled into a wave of change, and many bishops and leaders have been caught up in the conviction that church authority must be renewed to conform more closely to the biblical examples.

Now it is the Protestants' turn to study these questions as deeply. Protestants all recognize the need of leadership in the church, and whether they call their leaders bishops, presidents, chairmen, or moderators, they recognize them as shepherds and spokesmen for their churches when these men do in fact express the opinion of their churches. So "collegiality" is in a way an accepted fact among Protestants. Many Protestants would be willing to acknowledge a "senior bishop" on this sort of basis, a presiding bishop with an authority of prestige rather than juridical power, such as the bishop of Canterbury, for example. The idea of an international symbol of Christian unity would also not be unacceptable for many Protestants. Developments concerning these issues in years to come should be as interesting on the Protestant side as the Roman Catholic.

Most of this chapter on ministry and structure has been devoted to the nature of the church's ministry as it developed historically into various church offices. These questions of offices and structure will occupy center stage for a long time to come, both within and between churches. They are problems we must continually wrestle with to carry out the church's work in today's world.

But they certainly are not the only issues regarding the church's structure. It would be equally important to pose the question of each single congregation's structure. How can your congregation organize itself more efficiently to serve its community? How can the layman be incorporated more effectively into the church's work? Is money wisely spent building new showpiece church edifices when it could be used elsewhere? Perhaps a model for the ministry and structure of the future church can be seen in Kansas City, Missouri, where a church building was consecrated in 1968 which houses jointly Presbyterian, United, Episcopalian, and Roman Catholic congregations, eliminating many costly and inefficient duplications. The question of structure embraces these dimensions of local work too.

In conclusion, let me emphasize once again: *The real problem regarding ministry and structure is the question of mission.* Christians must never cease asking themselves, "What should the church be doing?" Only by probing this question will matters of ministry and structure fall into place, for we shall then adopt those structures necessary to fulfill our mission.

I shall close this chapter with a confession. In my former parish our church council met once a month, the usual practice. Our agenda was filled with items of everyday parish affairs and finances. Now that I think back on those rewarding years, I cannot remember ever putting the routine business aside to pose the really basic question, "What is it that we are really trying to do as a congregation in this community?" We had buried ourselves with secondary matters and skipped over the central question.

It may be that "the greatest hang-up in the church today is over structure." These problems of ministry, structure, and authority loom as imposing hurdles in the way to unity. Yet though we cannot now see clear light at the end of this tunnel, there is at least one source for optimism: we are considering these things together, trying to discover which structures best serve the church's mission today, and learning from one another in this search.

6.

Worship and Piety

> . . . disunity is as manifest in the differing ways
> of worship as in disagreements concerning doc-
> trines and institutions. Indeed it is at this point
> that disunity becomes explicit and the sense of
> separation most acute.[48]
> — Faith and Order Report

This category may prove to be the most troublesome obstacle to unity because we are dealing with the intangible style of life and worship which characterizes each church. It is an unwieldy topic and difficult to pin down. What would you reply, for example, to a man who opposes merger with another church by saying, "I can accept their doctrine and their way of organization, but I just do not feel at home with them"? One can grapple with concrete theological issues, but it is extremely hard to deal with this uneasiness toward churches of a totally different "feel."

Change and renewal can also be more difficult to accomplish in this area than in the other two. This is not surprising. The average layman is not keenly interested in the fine points of theological dialog. Nor is he overly aware of the intricacies of ecclesiastical structure. But the worship and piety of his church touch him very directly and personally. His faith is nurtured and he worships through the liturgy of the worship service. Theological currents and organizational changes will hardly be noticed, but introduce any major changes in the liturgy, and you will have provided a major topic for Sunday dinner conversation!

This is quite natural. We are, after all, creatures of habit. Our style of worship over the years takes deep root in our souls. In a different church we are distracted by all sorts of trifles. We can never find the proper page for the liturgy; we do not recognize the hymn melodies; and we are unsure when to sit and stand. In our own church we are "at home" with the prayers, music, chants, and responses we have known since childhood.

This fact struck me personally one Sunday many years ago in Germany. I had been worshipping in German churches where the theology was the same as in my home church, but the language, songs, and style of worship was different. One Sunday I was invited with some friends to a service on an American army base, and I found myself unexpectedly but deeply moved when the service began with those familiar words, "Beloved in the Lord! Let us draw near with a true heart. . . ." Thousands of miles from America I felt "at home" again.

It is no wonder then that the differences of worship and piety tend to keep us apart. It is no wonder that for the average Christian changes in this area are hard to accept.

But it is equally true that constant rethinking and renewal is as vital in this realm as in others. Our ways of worship and church life must be conditioned to our times and circumstances, and if we refuse to be open to these changes, the church will soon become a relic of past centuries. This does not mean that the church bends with every passing fad and fashion, but worship must be meaningful in a contemporary setting. The stately cadence of the King James Bible may be dear to many, but some of it is garble to a teenager and might well give him the impression that the whole Christian message is an old-fashioned vestige of the past.

So here is our problem. How can there be any unity in the church when the worship lives of various groups are so diverse? And how can all churches work together to renew their practice and piety in the world of today?

If we pause and reflect for a moment on "what worship is," we soon find that we are probing something which cannot be neatly bound into a definition. Worship is our response in praise, thanksgiving, and prayer to God. Through worship we both express our faith and are being nurtured in faith. We worship both as individuals and as the whole family of God. Worship can take place anywhere, at any time, and in limitless ways.

In analyzing worship we speak of "theological" and "cultural" factors. Since worship is an expression of faith, its form is determined by the theological convictions of our faith. Our theology finds its echo in our worship, and the way we worship must be harmonious with these convictions. For instance, we believe that man's first impulse standing before God is a trembling awareness of his own sinfulness, and that after confessing his transgressions he lifts his eyes to receive God's gracious forgiveness. From this theological viewpoint, it is logical to begin the worship service with a prayer of confession, followed by the words of absolution and grace. To make clear that we are praying to the triune God, we open the service "in the name of the Father, and of the Son, and of the Holy Ghost." One can follow right through the service and see that each part carries with it theological meaning.

The difference between the Roman Catholic mass and the Lutheran service with Communion — and they are basically the same service — comes largely from the theological objections of the reformers to parts of the Roman mass. One can figure out many of the theological disputes between the two groups simply by comparing the two services side-by-side, although the differences are not as apparent now after recent liturgical changes on both sides as they were in past centuries.

The words of our hymns also carry theological overtones. The great hymns like "A Mighty Fortress," "O God Our Help in Ages Past," and "Praise to the Lord the Almighty" are immortal not just because they are sung to inspiring melodies but because their theological vision is so solidly planted in praise to and trust in God. But the church is also plagued with hymns that concentrate more on the singer's well-being than on God, or which make God more a "buddy" than the sovereign Lord of the universe. The theology of these songs is little more than mushy sentimentalism. If a pastor or organist declines to sing them in church, it is not due to stubborn intolerance but because he judges such songs to be poor theological reflections of our faith.

One criterion for changes in worship is, does this new form better express our faith and our theological outlook? If such outward practices as standing around the altar are a better way of symbolizing the brotherhood and unity which Christ intended with the first Lord's Supper than kneeling in a row, it might be a worthwhile change. On the other hand, if kneeling as a sign of humble devotion and gratitude is more appropriate, it should be retained. We must constantly think about the theological meaning behind the way we worship.

Accepting diversity in worship does not mean indifference to these theological factors. Rather it means that we look at our liturgical services, songs, and forms, asking if they do in fact reflect good theology. But it also means that we not judge the liturgies of other churches by the narrow view of any one theological school or trend.

The "cultural" elements of worship are those imprints which every liturgy bears of its history, traditions, and national flavor. These factors are mixed with the theological content to give a liturgy its "feel" or peculiar personality. The official theology of a Swedish Lutheran congregation worshiping in the Uppsala cathedral and a Lutheran congregation in Midwestern America might be the same, but these other factors would result in the two services barely resembling one another.

Over the years these cultural heritages have given today's churches a wide variety of worship forms. Lutherans sing stately chorales, monks chant in Gregorian style, Pentecostals clap their hands to swinging gospel songs, and Presbyterians intone the Psalms. Some congregations listen quietly to the sermon, while others punctuate the preacher's words with "amens" and "halleluias" of their own. With the passing of time, one also finds many of these forms being adopted by other churches, especially in melting-pot America, where the Lutheran hymnbook and the Roman Catholic song books include hymns from many churches and traditions.

What a catastrophe it would be if we did not accept the need for such diversity in the church! How many missionary endeavors have crippled themselves by trying to force the cultural setting of European or American worship on an African tribe! The cultural elements of worship will vary with time and place, and it would be disastrous to press everyone into a uniform mold of worship.

Of course we do not applaud willy-nilly every innovation in worship that comes along. We must judge the cultural factors according to the standards of good taste and common sense. But in the end each church must find its own style of worship. Without such flexibility the church would soon be frozen into cast-iron rigidity.

It is rewarding to take a look at the worship and life of the New Testament church. There we find already those elements of worship common to our churches today, even though our glimpses into early worship are extremely sketchy. We catch a quick glance in the days immediately following Pentecost, when the believers praised God-in-Song; listened to the apostles' teaching, equivalent of today's scriptural readings and sermon; prayed; and broke bread together in a common meal celebrating the Lord's Last Supper, the forerunner of our Eucharist or Communion service (Acts 2:42, 46).

Certainly singing was a common feature of early Christian worship. The Jews sang, and Jesus sang with his disciples (Mark 14:26, Matt. 26:30). When the Christians were finally pushed out of the temple and synagogue, they retained much from Jewish worship, including singing (Acts 16:52; Eph. 5:19; Col. 3:16). Paul is probably quoting an early Christian hymn when he writes,

Awake O sleeper, and arise from the dead,
And Christ shall give you light (Eph. 5:14).

The sermon was certainly central to the New Testament church, both as a missionary proclamation to non-believers and to the worshipping community itself. The first recorded sermon in the Christian church is Peter's Pentecost address (Acts 2). All through the book of Acts we find the disciples proclaiming the message. The office of deacons was founded for the express purpose of allowing the apostles to devote more time to preaching (Acts 6:2).

Perhaps it is worth mentioning that long sermons and dozing listeners also have their early biblical precedent! Passing through Asia Minor, Paul stopped for a week at Troas and preached a Sunday evening sermon. We read in Acts 20 that Paul "prolonged his speech until midnight," so that the young man Eutychus "sank into a deep sleep as Paul talked still longer" and finally toppled out of a third story window!

The common meal assumed central importance. According to Paul's first letter to Corinth, chapter 11, the most extensive account we have of the New Testament Eucharist service, it was much more of a meal than the ritualized ceremony with the tiny dried wafer and barest sip of wine we now celebrate. When they "broke bread together" in the New Testament, it was a substantial meal (suggesting that Paul may well have found more "communion" and "eucharist" in our church basement potluck dinners than in our formal Communion service)! On the other hand, the emphasis we do give Holy Communion is consistent with New Testament worship.

Baptism was a key ritual in the early church, as it

is today. But today it presents one of the major ecumenical problems, since between infant baptism and adult baptism there is a fundamental and deep cleavage on what baptism is. It has been a subject of much study. But since most churches rejecting infant baptism also hold their distance from the ecumenical movement, there has been very little fruitful dialog on this point. But it will inevitably come.

So we find in the New Testament the first stages of those ingredients of our worship today. But even more important is the fact that in the early church — a single united church — there was never one uniform way of worship. The worship of the early church can be described as a "unity in diversity" or vice-versa a "diversity in unity." The report of the Worship Commission of Faith and Order at Montreal stated in 1963:

> There is in the New Testament a greater variety of forms and expressions of worship than in the majority of the divided churches and traditions today. On the other hand the unity is particularly striking, because it combines diversity of shape with concentration around a single heart, the source of its life and power.[44]

This living center of all worship is of course "the death and resurrection of Jesus Christ," and "the Holy Spirit is the energy which creates and preserves it."

This common faith was cohesive enough to allow development of diverse liturgical traditions without splintering the church. In the great centers of Christianity worship and church life evolved with their distinctive flavors, though the essential elements of worship ran as common threads through them all. We can trace the development of various Egyptian and Syrian liturgical families as the ancestors of much Orthodox liturgy. In the European church we have the "Gallican rites" and the "Ambrosian rite" among others, although with the emergence of Rome as the dominant influence in the West the "Roman rite" became the basis for the nearly uniform usage of the Roman Latin mass within Roman Catholicism.

There is an awesome diversity in Christian worship today. The formal, sacramental masses of the Orthodox and Roman Catholic worship are actually closely related, although on a Sunday morning they appear as only shirt-tail cousins. Add the Anglicans and Lutherans, who retained the basic structure of the Roman liturgy but "Protestantized" it. Continue further to the Reformed-Presbyterian tradition which eliminated the mass and reconstructed their own liturgies. Then consider the freer Methodist, Congregationalist, and Baptist services, which are less formal, until you come to the high-pitched emotional tone and spontaneity of the Pentecostals. Finally we include the Quakers, who originally shunned all liturgy in favor of impromptu impulses from the worshipers.

That is indeed a staggering amount of variety!

Add to this multi-colored liturgical picture another element, namely all the liturgical experimentation going on today in every church, the "modern liturgies," "folk masses," "rock masses," and others. Pastors, priests, and parishes everywhere are trying new forms, searching for more meaningful worship. Much of this experimentation takes place among the youth, and the reactions of those accustomed to a more dignified and familiar intonation of liturgy ranges — quite naturally — from encouraging, interested, uneasy, puzzled, suspicious, to shocked and incensed. Some of what goes on is somewhat "far out," and many churchmen suspect gimmickry and sensationalism. But the vast majority of liturgical experimentation today is done in a devout and joyful spirit of genuine contemporary worship.

Much of this change is simply a revision of outmoded language. The prose of much of our liturgy is not the language we use today, and many prefer to worship in the language they normally think and speak. "Thee" and "thou" give way to "you." Wooden expressions become more colloquial. One university chapel eliminated the traditional

> The Lord be with thee;
> And with thy spirit

in favor of

> May Jesus Christ live within you;
> And within you too, pastor.

Few would dispute the need for modern language. But there is room for discussion on which modern version is best suited for worship. The ideal is language that is understandable but not chummy, dignified but not stilted, and beautiful but not flowery.

Usually these new forms of worship are precisely that: new *forms*. Experimental groups keep the elements of worship but vary their form of expression. Instead of playing centuries-old hymns on the organ, they strum folk tunes on the guitar; for a monologue sermon they substitute a dialog between two or more persons or maybe a drama; instead of somber, colorless black and white pastors' robes they wear psychedelic, flower-patterned vestments to symbolize joy and celebration; rather than reading a biblical text, they might sing a song about the passage; instead of a stamped wafer they may use a loaf of bread for the

Lord's Supper (as Jesus did). They do not cease to pray a prayer of confession or thanksgiving, but they pray or sing it in a different fashion. The basic parts of the liturgy remain, but in a different, sometimes a *very* different, form.

Yet this diversity goes deeper than just a difference in forms. The Faith and Order Report makes clear that the "genuine variety in Christian worship is not so much a variety of *forms* as a variety of *types.*"

A mass by Palestrina is for example vastly different from Geoffrey Beaumont's "folk mass," but they are two "forms" of the very same "type" of worship. The same applies to a Protestant service of Communion and a Roman Catholic mass. But a Protestant Communion and a Protestant service without communion are two different types of worship. The *form* of the Eucharist is one question, but a more profound question is whether some other *type* of worship altogether might not be better in certain situations.

What type of worship can best express Christian devotion, celebrate God's presence, and bring to him our intercessions? This query brings us back to the very complex heart of the question, "What then is worship?" It embraces both the problem of forms and types as well as the theological consideration of worship.

Christian worship today revolves around two basic types of worship: the Roman Catholic and Orthodox mass comes to a climax with the Lord's Supper, whether in a great cathedral or in an "underground" mass in somebody's living room, and the Protestant service concentrates primarily on the preaching of the Word without the Eucharist. True, this is not a difference between black and white, since the Roman Catholic mass includes Scripture readings and homilies, and the Protestants celebrate the Lord's Supper as solemnly as Roman Catholics, if less frequently.

But the contrast is accurate, because it depicts both a historical and present difference in emphasis. The heart of Roman Catholic worship is the Eucharist, and of Protestant worship the Word. A Roman Catholic might not miss a sermon, but he would regard the mass as chopped off in the middle if there were no Communion. A Protestant would regard a service without a sermon as a sort of empty shell (though he might welcome its brevity).

This two-fold emphasis on Word and sacrament has its roots in church history. The first part of the liturgy in the ancient church was the "service of the Word," and was attended by all believers, confirmed or not. This included Scripture readings and a sermon. At its conclusion the non-confirmed "catechumens" left, and the second part, the "service of the Lord's Supper," was celebrated by the confirmed believers.

This led to the feeling that this second half was the really important part. In the old Roman Catholic scheme a believer could miss the first part of the mass, but if he arrived in time for the three bells announcing the start of the Eucharist service, he was counted as "present" for the mass. Present liturgical leaders of the Roman church are eager to jettison this old idea in favor of seeing the entire service as a whole, but from a historical point of view one can see how this mentality evolved.

The Reformation emphasized the proclamation of God's grace and man's response of faith. This shifted the liturgical weight to the Word, although the balance between Word and sacrament is different in various churches. The Anglicans tend to have both a "preaching service" and a "service of the Eucharist" on a

Sunday morning. Many Lutherans retained every Sunday Communion until centuries after the Reformation, though monthly Communion services are the usual pattern today. The Reformed and free church traditions often celebrate the Lord's Supper even less frequently.

The Roman Catholic feeling is something like this: if the Lord's Supper is the high point of Christian worship, a liturgical service is incomplete without it. Most Protestants would perhaps summarize their position this way: if a believer receives the Lord's Supper about once a month, why not have a monthly service for the whole congregation together instead of weekly celebrations where only a fourth of the worshipers commune? (This would lead us to the next question, "How often should one commune?" but that goes beyond the bounds of this study.)

Both Protestants and Roman Catholics recognize that their respective traditions have tended to be one-sided. To be a "church of the Word" or a "church of the sacrament" is too narrow. Christian worship and piety must embrace both in their fullness. Today there is an awareness on all sides that "Word" and "sacrament" are closely intertwined with each other. At the Ecumenical Institute in Strasbourg, France, we held a seminar on this theme "Gospel and Sacrament." Among the conclusions of more than forty Roman Catholic and Protestant theologians from all over the world was this:

> The antagonism between Gospel (Word) and Sacrament which dominated western Christian theology must be replaced by a more fundamental concept of Gospel *and* Sacrament.[45]

This means that in these very basic questions theologians of all churches are studying together instead of against each other. They are all examining the relation of Word and sacrament. They are all probing the meaning of sacrament and symbol in worship. The results of such study will not filter down into our Sunday services for a long time, but they will have profound long-term effects upon our church life. Certainly we shall all profit from a deeper understanding of worship.

This whole question of the relation between Word and sacrament is but one aspect of the problem, "What then *is* worship?" There are many other questions as well. Many doubt the worth of formal congregational services altogether and would prefer to worship in somebody's living room with a dozen or so others. Many Protestants have held such "cell group" devotions for years, and there is a growing movement among Roman Catholics for similar small, informal masses.

Another type of worship which would be of enormous value and which is being encouraged in many churches is family worship by the father in a short daily devotion. This practice gives direct expression to the "priesthood of all believers," enriching not only the family's faith but the family itself. This is but one example of a kind of worship beside our regular Sunday format; there are countless others, as the Christian church is ever searching for renewal in worship.

It is perhaps impossible for us to issue any conclusive verdict on new liturgical developments. We can only use our best judgment and rely on the passage of time to iron out the edges. In our attempts to find a "meaningful" way of worship we run the risk of narrowing the breadth of the liturgy to our own tastes.

A "meaningful" liturgy in a university crowd might appear weird in a parish congregation. A Roman Catholic writer notes that the addition of literary readings in the mass would be meaningful to him, then adds:

> But what of the plane geometry teacher next to me? The stenographer? The milkman? The judge? the housewife?... Thus the problem... The church exists for the college teacher and the cab driver simultaneously.[46]

Those new trends which lack wide-spread meaning will pass from the scene in time, or remain limited to those groups which find them significant.

The church stands in the middle of the clash between ancient liturgical traditions and new ideas. It must take the 20th century into its liturgical life, just as every age has left its imprint on the development of liturgy. Consider how many songs Luther literally pulled in off the street to make hymns. Some of the liturgical footprints of our century will survive, and many more will expire with the passing of time. But the church can never ignore the present age in its worship.

Yet on the other side, those ways of worship which have served for centuries can hardly be discarded lightly. There is a magnificent continuity in Christian worship, a richness in knowing that I am praying the very prayers uttered by Augustine, Francis of Assisi, Thomas Aquinas, Luther, and others. When we sing the three-fold "kyrie" or the "sanctus" of the Eucharist our voices blend with the echoes of voices throughout the ages. The Lord's Prayer unites us in spirit with the disciples on that day when our Lord taught it to them, and through Aaron's benediction ("The Lord bless you and keep you . . .") we stand with those receiving

God's blessing in the wilderness after the Exodus. Treasures like these are ageless. Their language and musical form might change, but they continue with the universal church.

These last few paragraphs serve to summarize this complex, delicate and urgent problem of worship. Everyone would agree that it is necessary to preserve what is essential and precious, yet equally necessary to change with the times and discontinue what is no longer needed, but very likely no two people in the world would agree on exactly what belongs in the first category and what in the second!

But let us close this chapter on a note of unity. The fact that within all churches there is a growing interest and variety in worship will help us realize more easily that diversity in worship need not cause church division. One of the features of this liturgical development today is that churches are learning and borrowing from one another. Churches that had abandoned historic liturgical practices are now incorporating many traditional elements into revised liturgies. Other churches that have inherited fixed liturgies and passive congregations are becoming more informal and involving their lay people in worship. I am reminded of one of my indignant laymen who thought it was unfair of the Roman Catholics not only to start singing hymns but "our good Protestant hymns as well, even 'A Mighty Fortress' !"

It is good to recall the early church, where home-made liturgies were sprouting up everywhere, but where the church remained one in its Lord. If we too grasp this overarching oneness in Christ, it is not difficult to recognize the need for diversity in worship, and we can evaluate other liturgical forms and our own without shattering our bond of fellowship. Lukas

Vischer posed this question in the Faith and Order Report:

> ... starting on the basis of the new consciousness of unity which has been reached in the ecumenical movement, can we not return to the attitude of the ancient church and not only *endure* the same diversity of worship forms, but even *affirm* it? [47]

It is of course humanly impossible to expect that a person would feel at home or even worshipful with all these different ways of worship. But it is the goal of ecumenism that Christians will accept the need for such diversity and even be willing to participate in occasional experiments in worship. We might continue to be mystified at a Russian Orthodox mass, ill at ease at a Pentecostal revival meeting, and perhaps irritated at a folk mass, but recognizing our oneness in Christ we shall have taken a big and very important step ahead.

7.

Toward the Year A.D. 2000

> We must always come back to the central problem
> of the ecumenical debate: what is Christianity?
> Each individual church, each Christian communion,
> must ask this question when it examines itself, its
> history, its ecumenical relations, its belief, mission,
> structure, liturgy and organic life, and when it re-
> news its consecration to the sole service of the
> glory of the Lord with its whole heart and mind.[46]
>
> — Bernard Lambert, O.D.

What lies ahead for ecumenism? No one can predict
what the church will be by the end of this century
The church of the year A.D. 2000 is indeed "the church
nobody knows" today.

Thus far in this book I have used the word "ecumenism" in its usual sense of referring to relations between
churches. The ecumenical picture of the year A.D.
2000 will depend on the development of this level
of ecumenism, but it will be even more profoundly
formed by two other levels of ecumenism.

If we draw a circle to represent the ecumenism
between churches, we must draw within this circle
another smaller circle, which stands for the renewal
taking place within individual churches. Then we must
draw a larger circle around both circles, representing

the ecumenism of the churches with the whole world. "The church nobody knows" of the year A.D. 2000 will be determined by events in all three of these circles.

The ecumenical movement derives both its unpredictability and its hope from the smallest circle. Each and every church today is confronted with new problems arising from the modern world, and churchmen in every denomination are grappling with fundamental and urgent questions of their own church's existence —doctrine, mission, structure, ministry, worship. Within every church there is a desire for renewal and rededication to the tasks that face us. Because the church must adapt itself to the radically new situation of this world, we all know that if we survive until the end of this century, our own church will be quite different in A.D. 2000. A church closed to renewal will endure until A.D. 2000 only as a fossil, if at all.

It is only on the basis of renewal that ecumenism is possible at all. A person smugly satisfied with everything his church is doing and not willing to budge one inch will hardly be enthusiastic for expanding contacts with other churches. His idea of ecumenism is, "if everyone would agree with me and join my church, we would be united." But an individual who is anxious that his church adapt its mission to the new situations in urban and technological societies cannot help but be drawn closer to those of other churches who feel the same concern.

Since the problem facing the church and the need for renewal are shared by us all, the renewal going on within each church automatically furnishes a powerful impulse for ecumenism. Our reactions to most of the really crucial issues before us are not predetermined by our squabbles of the past, so that as we devote increasing attention to these present and future questions, our past divisions fade into the background. We are drawn together by the urgency of current challenges. It is no wonder that the younger generation chafes with impatience at theologians who are absorbed with the problems of the past.

In a sense, even the ecumenical movement as we think of it—churches drawing together—is passé, of only secondary importance. Ecumenism is no longer primarily the task of two or more churches coming closer, but far more importantly the task of all churches reaching forward toward a renewed church of the future. Our usual picture of ecumenism is of two people or two sides facing each other in discussion, but a more accurate image would be all of us walking together side-by-side facing the work of the years to come. In every major merger negotiation going on today, the basic question is never, "How can we adjust and combine our two set-ups to fit together?," but rather the common question, "What form should the church assume to carry out its mission most effectively?"

Many Protestants have been and still are suspicious of Roman Catholic ecumenism on the grounds that behind the friendly facade Rome is really working toward reunion as "return" or "conversion" to Rome. This was true of the past, and even today what loyal Roman Catholic does not feel that the true center of the organized Christian church is the bishop of Rome? When the archbishop of Canterbury met with Pope John XXIII — the first meeting in history between the leaders of the two churches — the pope read Archbishop Fisher part of a speech he had given in English, which included a reference to the "time when our separated brethren should return to the Mother

Church." Dr. Fisher interrupted to reply, "Your Holiness, not *return*." The pope was puzzled and asked, "Not return? Why not?" The Anglican leader answered, "None of us can go backwards. We are each running in parallel courses; we are looking forward until, in God's good time, our two courses approximate and meet." After a moment's pause the pope responded, "You are right."

In Roman Catholicism the accent has shifted decidedly from reunion as "return" to reunion as "renewal." At the time of the second Vatican Council Pope John spoke unapologetically about the reunion of all churches to Rome, but he did so in the conviction that his church needed an inner renewal. Part of his reason for summoning the council was to accelerate this renewal within the Roman church, which would in turn serve the wider purpose of eventual reunion.

The very process of dialog itself brings about change and renewal. When a John Birch society member harangues and argues with a radical SDS youth, each shouts with no intention of listening or learning from the other. But in true dialog, where partners trust each other and are open to learn from the other, one cannot help but gain new insights and new ways of seeing things. This is true whether the dialog is between Protestant and Protestant, Protestant and Roman Catholic, Republican and Democrat, Christian and Communist, or any other combination. To those who say that neither Roman Catholics nor Protestants will change, Robert McAfee Brown replies:

> . . . in the course of the ecumenical encounter, the Catholic church will be changed as well as the Protestant churches. . . . The Catholic, as he looks

to what his church will be fifty years from now,
need not believe he will find there an exact replica
of what he sees today. For the church will have
engaged in far-reaching inner reform, partly as a
result of the ecumenical dialogue. It will even have
gained certain things from the best of Protestantism, just as in the interval Protestantism will have
gained from the best of Catholicism.[49]

Thus the dialog between churches cannot help but
be a strong force for renewal within each church. The
end result of all this ongoing reformation and renewal
might be unpredictable, but on it rests our hopes for
the church of tomorrow.

The largest circle encompasses not just the churches
but the whole world. It signifies a larger dimension of
ecumenism which has captured the vision of many
ecumenists today: the unity of the church not only
within its own members but with the whole world.
It represents a change from ecumenism as an inner-
churchly affair to ecumenism as the church's true
mission in the world. To use an athletic metaphor
(the kind St. Paul liked too): rather than scrimmaging
among its own team, ecumenism must now move on
to the big stadium, confronting the outside world
with its message of brotherhood, fellowship, and reconciliation.

Ecumenism has come around full circle to the original meaning of the word *oikumene*, "the whole in-
habited world." The message of unity and reconciliation is intended not only for relations between
churches — it is the very message the churches bring
to a troubled world.

We call this widest circle "secular ecumenism,"
because it symbolizes the church's outreach to the

whole secular world. Thanks to a renaissance of theological consideration of the secular world, the church has been re-awakened to its task in the world. More and more churchmen have come to see that the church is not just an institution, not just an organization to nurture its own members, but it is an arm of *service to the entire world.* God is present and active in all his creation, and the church must follow wherever it discerns the hand of God in world affairs. It is God's own Son who has patterned the blueprint with his own life: "... even as the Son of Man came not to be served but to serve, and to give his life ..." (Matt. 20:28).

What is the church supposed to do in this world? Bring the message of forgiveness and reconciliation to God in Christ. Not only preach it, but live it. And just as Christ brought this message to those outside the pale of established religion — Mary Magdalene, Zacchaeus, the Roman ruler, the Samaritan and Greek women—so the church moves out into the secular world to proclaim and to make actual this news: the bitterness and hostility between men and God and among men have been overcome by Christ and can be replaced by brotherhood and love. Into teeming urban slums, underdeveloped areas, pockets of poverty, hostile neighborhoods, and all other places of human indignity, the church moves to bring reconciliation and healing as a shaft of light into a darkened world.

Scholars of all denominations are calling the church to come out of its cocoon and minister to the secular world. And since this ministry is the same for all denominations, churches are banding together in growing cooperation in these areas. This secular ecumenism is known by other names as well. To emphasize its thrust of service, some call it "pastoral" or "practical" ecumenism, while others indicate its concern for the whole world with the name "the wider ecumenism."

Whatever its name, this dimension of ecumenism throws the traditional ecumenism between churches into an entirely new perspective. For one thing, the inherited differences of the past no longer appear so formidable to churchmen who are sharing a common ministry in the world, working together as brother Christians. Such persons take unity for granted, because they have found unity in this service they consider so essential. They show little interest for the doctrinal problems which linger between them. Secondly, secular ecumenism exposes the church's divisions as the disgraceful and shameful scandals they are. How can the Christian church bear witness to the world of the forgiveness and mercy of God creating brotherhood among men when it is so full of divisions, mistrust, and dissensions within itself?

The church's involvement in the secular world is a topic for much study. But no matter which of many views one takes, the vast majority of Christians realize that the church must reach out into the secular world. And this larger circle of secular, pastoral, or wider ecumenism is certain to provide stimulus to ecumenism between churches. Not only does it incorporate ecumenism into the church's mission outreach, but it urges us to more intense ecumenical efforts between churches by laying bare the hypocritical duplicity of churches who proclaim "peace, peace" to the world when there is no peace even among its own members.

The church of tomorrow will be shaped by all three of these concentric circles: renewal within each church, improving relations among churches, and the church's witness to the whole world. Each of these levels is interposed on the other two. "One Church Renewed for Mission" was the theme of the British Conference on Faith and Order in 1964, and it has remained in my memory because that marvelous five-word phrase summarizes the whole scope of these three circles. Ecumenism embraces this entire task.

As Fr. Lambert writes at the beginning of this chapter, at the heart of ecumenism is the most fundamental question of them all, "What is Christianity?" The ecumenical movement causes and is in turn nurtured by renewal, growing fellowship, and outreach to the world. In this sense, ecumenism is not just part of the church's task: it *is* the church's task in the years to come.

But the most important factor is one that stands above all these three circles — the guiding hand of God's Spirit. "The more I reflect on the problem of church unity," wrote the late Cardinal Saliege of Toulouse, France, "I know that the solution depends on the action of the Holy Spirit in our souls." [50] Whatever the church of A.D. 2000 will be, its architect and builder will be the Spirit of God. Church organizations will creak along, committees will meet interminably, scholars will write books — and the end result will be the product of the Spirit's hand behind all these endeavors.

"But the Holy Spirit is calling every Christian, not only the professional theologians but every member of the people of God, to cooperate with him." [51] We are all part of the ecumenical movement, from the church leaders who bear direct responsibility for their churches to the laypeople striving to be Christians in this world and to improve the bond of fellowship with their neighbors from different churches.

Ecumenism on the local level is lagging well behind

other levels. Henry P. van Dusen, past president of Union Theological Seminary, makes this sharp observation of the ecumenical movement:

> Today, Christian unity is most advanced and strongest where one would expect unity to be the most difficult to achieve and maintain — on the world scene; least vital where it should be easiest and inevitable — in villages and towns and cities.[52]

He continues by remarking that the ecumenical leaders of international committees know each other better and trust each other more than ministers in most local communities. The decade of the 1970s should be a period for "grass roots" ecumenism to catch up with national and international progress. This means that the key person in the ecumenical movement now is not really the church official but *you,* the reader of this book, in your own congregation and community.

Yet one last word, for anybody who still might doubt that he has a part to play in ecumenism. We all need to pray. We must pray for our own church, for other churches, and for the whole church on earth. The great French ecumenist Yves Congar once said, "The threshold of ecumenism can only be crossed on one's knees." [53] At the close of the Vatican Council Pope Paul invited all non-Roman observers to a joint service of prayer at St. Paul's-Outside-the-Walls in December, 1965. At this last official meeting with council observers the pope closed his sermon with the words, "And now let us all pray together. . . ."

The ship symbolizing the ecumenical movement sails on into the uncharted waters of the future. Some problems will melt away, other previously unsolvable issues will be solved, and some problems might become sharper. But we live in an exciting age of knowing that the future holds great hope for change and renewal. As we pray and work in the Spirit for the greater unity of the church, "the church nobody knows" will take shape as a church where indeed, in the words of that first Christian creed, "Jesus is Lord."

NOTES

1. *A Time for Unity,* London: SCM Press, 1964, p. 35.
2. Paragraph 2. Documents from the second Vatican Council are quoted from *The Documents of Vatican II,* ed. by Walter M. Abbott, S.J., New York: The America Press, 1966.
3. The standard reference work is *A History of the Ecumenical Movement,* ed. by Ruth Rouse and Stephen Neill. Briefer accounts can be found in *The Ecumenical Revolution* by Robert McAfee Brown, *Two Centuries of Ecumenism* by George E. Tavard, *One Great Ground of Hope* by Henry P. van Dusen, as well as many others.
4. Barrett McGurn, *A Reporter Looks at American Catholicism,* New York: Hawthorn Books, 1967, p. 218f.
5. *Op. cit.,* p. 34.
6. *Toward an Undivided Church,* New York: Association Press, 1967, p. 49.
7. *Op. cit.,* p. 30f.
8. Peter Nichols, *Politics of the Vatican,* London: Pall Mall Press, 1968, p. 109.
9. *One Great Ground of Hope,* Philadelphia: The Westminster Press, 1961, p. 149.
10. *One in Christ,* Philadelphia: Muhlenberg Press, 1957, p. 40f.
11. G. D. Kilpatrick, *Remaking the Liturgy,* London: Collins, Fontana Books, 1967, p. 7.
12. *Catholic Theology in Dialogue,* New York: Harper & Brothers, 1961, p. 76.
13. *Eucharist as Sacrifice,* New York, 1967, p. 196.
14. Article 7. The *Augsburg Confession* is quoted from *The Book of Concord,* ed. by Theodore G. Tappert, Philadelphia: Muhlenberg Press, 1959.

15. *The Social Sources of Denominationalism,* Cleveland: The World Publishing Company, 10th printing, 1967, p. 6.

16. Bernard Lambert, O.P., *Ecumenism—Theology and History,* New York: Herder and Herder, 1967, p. 141.

17. *Revelation,* 9.

18. *Ibid., 8.*

19. *Ibid., 24.* Not only Protestants but also many Roman Catholics were disappointed when Pope Paul insisted upon a traditional note by inserting the sentence, ". . . it is not from sacred Scripture alone that the church draws her certainty about everything which has been revealed." *Ibid.,* 9.

20. Francis Simons, *Infallibility and the Evidence.*

21. *An American Dialogue,* with Robert McAfee Brown, New York: Doubleday & Company, Anchor Books, 1961, p. 141.

22. Hans Küng, *Justification,* New York: Thomas Nelson & Sons, 1964, p. xx.

23. *Op. cit.,* p. 30.

24. *Ecumenism,* 22.

25. Jacques Dournes, in *Concilium,* Vol. 1, No. 4, p. 42.

26. *Ibid.,* p. 12.

27. *Ecumenism,* 11.

28. *The Documents of Vatican II,* op. cit., p. 715.

29. October 19, 1968, p. 345.

30. Matt. 16:16; 17:4, 17; John 18:10; 21:15; Acts 1:15; 2:14.

31. Romans 12; 1 Cor. 1:3, 8; 5:7; 16; 2 Cor. 13, etc.
    Today, April, 1968, p. 77.

32. 1 Tim. 3:1, 2, 8; 5:17. See Titus 1:5, 7.

33. *Authority in the Church,* New York: Sheed and Ward, 1966, p. 76.

34. "Shape and Style of the Church Tomorrow," in *Theology Today,* April, 1968, p. 77.

35. *The Church in the Next Decade,* New York: Macmillan, 1966, p. 128.

36. Stephan Mayor, in *The Scottish Journal of Theology,* March, 1968, p. 52.

37. p. 5.

38. p. 97

39. In *Unitas, Autumn,* 1967, p. 171.

40. Robert McAfee Brown, *The Ecumenical Revolution,* Garden City: Doubleday, 1967, p. 293.

41. *A Practical Guide to Ecumenism,* New York: Paulist Press, 1967, p. 148.
42. In *Unitas,* Summer, 1967, p. 126.
43. Faith and Order Report, Lund, 1952.
44. Faith and Order Paper No. 39, p. 11.
45. *Oecumenica* 1970, p. 263.
46. Richard E. DiLallo, in *America,* December 21, 1968, p. 651
47. *Op. cit.,* p. 75.
48. *Op. cit.,* p. 181.
49. *Op. cit.,* p. 80.
50. *Documentation Catholique,* January 22, 1956, col. 97f.
51. John B. Sheerin, C.S.P., *Op. cit.,* p. 170
52. *Op. cit.,* p. 111.
53. *Unitas,* Winter, 1967, p. 305

AUTHOR

Michael Rogness served for three years as a staff member of the Institute for Ecumenical Research, Strasbourg, France. He is a graduate of Luther Seminary, St. Paul, Minnesota. His doctorate in Reformation history is from the University of Erlangen, Germany. He is the author of *Melanchthon: Reformer Without Honor* (Augsburg, 1969). He served as a parish pastor and was on the teaching staff of St. Olaf College and Luther Seminary. Dr. Rogness is now pastor of First Lutheran Church, Duluth, Minnesota.

Date Due